Fascinating Alaska

Inhale the Essence

Acknowledgements

My heart felt thanks to my son Douglas, my wife Elaine, my granddaughter Jaime, my family & friends. Also to Joyce Boonlorn, Father Gerald, Joyce Clark, and Cindy Caserta. Their constructive encouragement helped make this book a success in good reading.

Editing by Joyce Boonlorn
Cover designed by Chris Tingom

Published by: Fascinating Alaska Publishing Co.
Book design by: Tina Wallace, Todd Communications
Print brokering by: Todd Communications
Distribution by: Todd Communications
Anchorage, Alaska
Artwork: Illustrations by Elaine Elbert, Denny Macom, Sean Young, Kurt Labonte, and Russ Mitchell.

Contents

1. Preface - My Alaska 6
2. Getting to Know Alaska 8
3. Captivating Adventures 14
4. My First Trip Hooked Me on Alaska 29
5. Winter on the Edge of the Bering Sea 36
6. Whaling in the Arctic 43
7. Josephine, the Friendly Moose 48
8. Vitalize Your Alaskan Experience 58
9. More Captivating Adventures 65
10. Life in the Village of Kalskag 86
11. Celebrating Slavic in Kalskag 91
12. We Traveled the Road Less Traveled 96
13. A Tale of Two Brothers 112
14. Alaska Has Captivated our Hearts 123
15. Facts & Figures 135
16. The Harsh Winters 141
17. The Long Awaited Summers 143
18. Awesome Wildlife 146
19. Northern Humor 151
20. Alaskan Tall Tales 155
21. Wisdom of a Survivor 163
22. The Gospel According to a Sourdough ... 164
23. The Sourdough Quiz 165
24. The Alaska Blessing 167
25. The Author 168

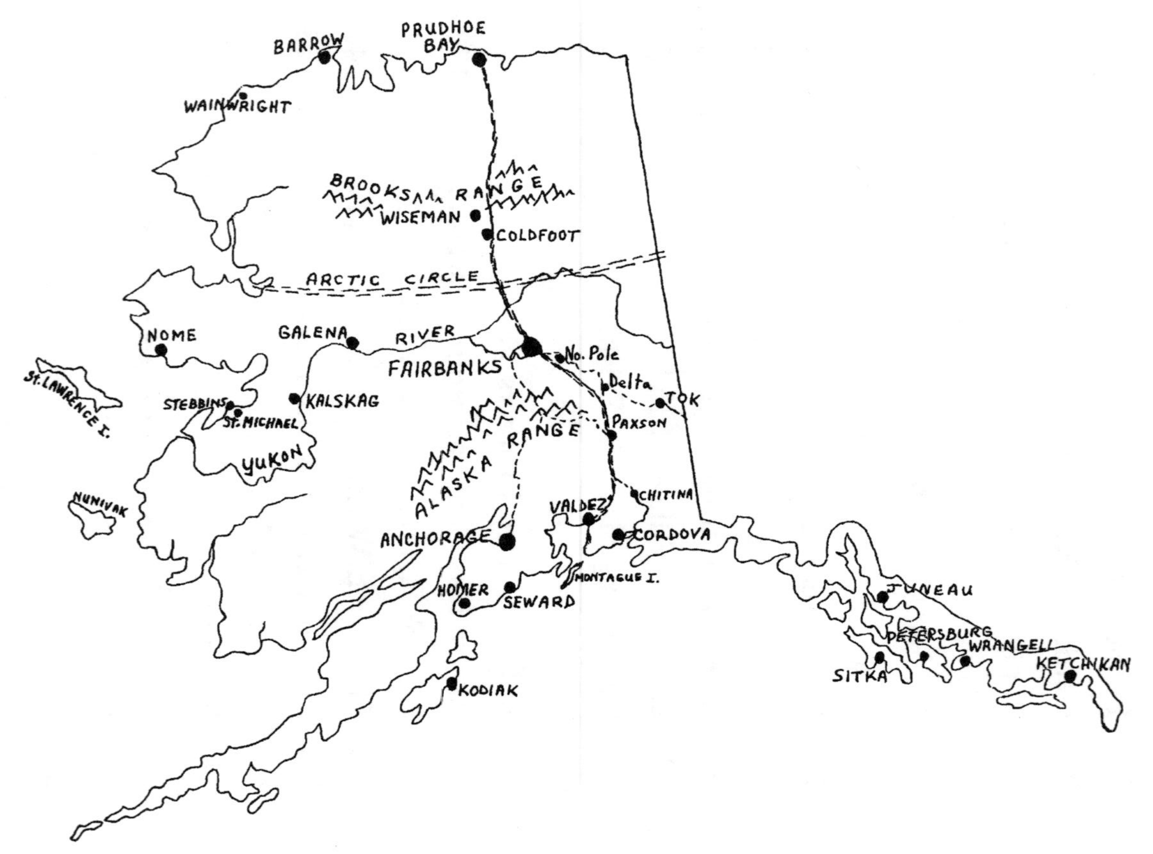

BARROW
PRUDHOE BAY
WAINWRIGHT
BROOKS RANGE
WISEMAN
COLDFOOT
ARCTIC CIRCLE
NOME
GALENA
RIVER
FAIRBANKS
No. Pole
Delta
TOK
St. LAWRENCE I.
STEBBINS
St. MICHAEL
KALSKAG
PAXSON
ALASKA RANGE
YUKON
NUNIVAK
CHITINA
VALDEZ
CORDOVA
ANCHORAGE
MONTAGUE I.
HOMER
SEWARD
KODIAK
JUNEAU
PETERSBURG
WRANGELL
SITKA
KETCHIKAN

The Author's Invitation

Alaska is more than a place to visit–it is a place to experience. Come and share the hospitality and the lifestyle that is Alaska. We are all travelers in the wilderness of life, and Alaskans find that the path is smoother when we share our adventures with friends.

I invite you to read some highlights of my 52 years under the northern skies, plus gripping stories of other folks who claim Alaska as their home. Then it will be your turn to venture out, witness the many interesting sights, and search for your very own experience.

Between the covers of this book you'll discover what it's really like to live on the Last Frontier, and get a truer sense of Alaska's wonders, its cruelty, and its magic.

With Warm Wishes

Don Elbert

My Alaska

By Don Elbert

I love living in My Alaska. This land is a prize piece of the Master's handiwork. The incomparable beauty and richness of the north has me under a spell. There is magic here that radiates into its inhabitants. Here I can soak in the morning sun as it rises up between the cleavage of two snow-covered mountain peaks. My senses bask in the splendor of majestic mountain ranges sculpted by God and polished by thousands of years' exposure to nature's raw forces. I envision tons of vanilla ice cream gently dropped across the land from a giant scoop by unseen heavenly hands.

Looking to the skies, I witness the pregnant clouds burst out to deliver their frosty contents. Crystal-shaped snowflakes paint the night white as they flutter down and tuck in this land under a white blanket.

Fall's icy blue skies alert me. Winter is coming on. Zipping up my parka, I step out into the cool, frosty breath of the Arctic wind. Listening intently to the earth's great stillness, I hear the crunching of snow under my boots. Alaska is an unpolluted land with a crisp, clean atmosphere. Breathing is easy here. Out in the bush, in the great all alone, there is a tremendous sense of serenity, peace and oneness with creation.

A warm feeling of enchantment gladdens my heart to look out over the open tundra and witness Mother Nature sleeping peacefully. She lays adorned in all her winter finery, silent under a fresh layer of winter frosting.

Bright flashes awaken the nights. I glance up to witness a phenomenon. The sky parts, like the Red Sea. There is a wall of darkness on the left and a wall of darkness on the right. The luster of the Aurora Borealis emblazons the sky, prancing in colored cadence, dancing like a lace curtain in a windstorm.

Filled with anticipation, I await the day winter awakes from her long sleep. With open arms I reach out and welcome the freshness of spring. The sun's warm rays melt the ice and snow and defrost the air we breathe. It is a joy to watch the darkness of winter ease into 24 hours of daylight. Blueberries ripen to a dark purple and fishing is abundant for man and bears. Which makes us both happy. The warm sun is like the warmth of Alaska's people, reflecting a love that is always in season, where laughter and friends are always welcome. Silent, cherished memories of the people who live here are the threads that unite us. For me, home is where my heart is, here in <u>My Alaska</u>.

<u>*Getting to Know Alaska*</u>

Alaska is a powerful and captivating attraction, calling to everyone. From the beauty of our mountain ranges with glistening snowcapped peaks, to the icebergs calving and plunging into the sea, the glory of nature is unforgettable. In the picturesque Arctic wonderland that moose, bears, caribou and other hardy creatures call home, you can breathe in the morning air and smell the freshness of the tundra and the newness of the day.

Alaska's lifestyle captures restless imaginations and leads to new experiences in life. One must see and feel this land to appreciate its richness and golden opportunities. The remoteness, freedom, and beauty of Alaska is available for all to experience.

"To the lover of pure wildness, Alaska is one of the most wonderful countries in the world," wrote the famed naturalist John Muir in the late 1800s. This famous quote came from his impression of the glaciers, forests, and vast expanses of unexplored territory when he sailed north through the Inside Passage. One hundred years later, his observation is still true. Less than one tenth of one percent of Alaska's landmass has been cleared or settled.

To the seasoned sourdough, Alaska is majestic. The magic glistens in our hearts like nuggets at the bottom of a gold pan. As one transitions from cheechako to sourdough, the harsh climate can indeed be forbidding, but it is not unlivable. Something special happens in our soul that we treasure when we adopt Alaska as our own.

Discover Alaska through the eyes of its people, and learn the secrets of why they live on the Last Frontier. You will also discover that the next best thing to living in Alaska is visiting.

The Mystique that was Alaska

And the Pioneers who Came North

When U.S. Secretary of State William H. Seward agreed to buy Alaska in 1867 for almost two cents an acre, many Americans opposed the purchase calling Alaska "Seward's Folly" and "Seward's Icebox."

This image of Alaska began to change in the late 1800s and early 1900s. It started when men came north to answer the call of the wild and solved the mystery of how to live and survive in these harsh conditions. They had to adapt to one of the world's coldest and cruelest climates in an inhospitable land.

Cheechako is what they were called, the men and women who came north looking for a fresh start at life in this raw and remote land. Cheechako (pronounced chee-cha-ko) is a newcomer to Alaska, a tenderfoot or greenhorn, someone who hasn't been here long. Most authorities agree that cheechako came into the English from Chinook Jargon, consisting of chee-"new" plus chako-"come." Some folks hang onto a more colorful version, believing that the name originated from folks arriving from Chicago. Native Alaskans had trouble pronouncing "Chicago" and the word that came out sounded like "cheechako." With age and wisdom, the cheechako advanced to the status of "sourdough" by facing the never-ending challenges placed on them and surviving in the Last Frontier.

Sourdoughs are the pioneers and prospectors, the residents who have spent most of their lives here. The name came from a yeasty starter, used to leaven bread and pancakes. The miners carried sourdough with them as they came north on foot during the famous Klondike Gold Rush in 1898. It became a staple, the basis for their "staff of life," and the name stuck to the pioneers who stayed all winter and used it.

In most cases, Alaska brought out the best in the men and women who came to accept the challenge of her call. They came full of ambition and courage to carve a life out of the bleak and barren wilderness. They were survivors. They helped tame this wild country, and in doing so they had to endure many hardships. They had to be resourceful and improvise, make do with what they had or do without. It was truly survival of the fittest and the weak became strong or they didn't survive.

A few sourdoughs were cantankerous, even antisocial, just like a few folks in any town. Some folks tease that sourdough means you're sour on Alaska but have no dough to leave, and that's true of a few who have fallen on hard times.

Why Men Came

Men first came north for the abundant prime furs found in Alaska. Then there was heard the most enticing word: gold. When news of this filtered down to the rest of the world the quest for gold began, causing a human flood to the Northland. Thousands came to Alaska seeking their fortune, dreaming of striking it rich because "thar's gold in them thar hills and streams." Many of our residents today are smitten with a fever that no doctor can cure, and it's called "Gold Fever."

The Fairbanks Exploration Company, during the years 1928-1958, operated eight gold dredges in this area. Just one of them, Gold Dredge #8, took in seven million ounces of gold from Goldstream in its 30 years of operation.

Goldrushes: Juneau 1880's, 40-mile country 1890's, Klondike Gold Rush 1896-1899, Circle City 1893, Nome 1898, Fairbanks 1902. Many miners followed these goldrushes, and small and large towns sprang up wherever gold was discovered.

The great depression of the 1930's devastated scores of people who lost everything they owned. Many, however, heard of the farming opportunities in Alaska's fertile

Matanuska Valley and the federal crop subsidies offered. They welcomed a chance to come north to start life anew.

In early March of 1942 the U.S. War Department, realizing the strategic importance of Alaska, sent thousands of military personnel north to build the Alaska Highway (then called the Alcan or the Alaska-Canada Highway). To speed up the building of the road, the Army took the path of least resistance instead of following the survey markers. This added more mileage and sharper twists and turns. The 1,500-mile Alcan was built in eight months and 12 days under some of the most horrendous conditions in an alien land. The Alaska section of the road was built by the all-black 97th Division of the Corps of Engineers.

One southern soldier said, "We knew we might freeze to death, so we took precautions. Those northern boys thought they could 'bulldoze' the weather and they froze their fingers, and their toes, and their ears."

Another soldier said about the highway, "It's miles and miles of nothing but miles and miles."

Despite the many lives lost during the construction of the Alcan, the highway forged ahead against great odds, and at great cost, to become a great success. Today, 57 years later it is still in use, the sole land link connecting Alaska to the lower 48 states.

During World War II, federal money and jobs brought thousands of construction workers and military personnel north for the building of military bases, aircraft runways, roads and housing. After completion of these projects, many discovered opportunities in Alaska and stayed, creating a rapid rise in population.

Statehood in 1959 sparked the natural curiosity of quite a

number of Americans and foreigners, and many began to travel to the 49th State to discover its beauty and enchantment.

Some came wanting only to be a part of the adventure that is Alaska, the Last Frontier, with its vastness and beauty.

Some came to get away from life in the big cities of the Lower 48, with noisy crowds and traffic, and take up a slower and more peaceful pace of existence.

Alaska attracts self-sufficient, independent souls. Some came to lead a subsistence lifestyle, living off the land, rivers and sea.

Still others came looking for a new start in life on free land, their land. For example, the Homestead Act provided the adventurous with a 160-acre parcel of land– theirs just for living on and planting crops.

A few came to escape from the law or alimony payments in the Lower 48.

With the huge discovery at Prudhoe Bay in 1968, the word went out again, but this time the word was oil, "black gold." The quest for jobs and riches again brought people north by the thousands to help build and work on the 800-mile pipeline, or to labor in the oilfields at Prudhoe Bay.

Captivating Adventures

I Didn't Want This Sea Lion in My Kitchen

By Randy Moore

Her body trembled as she shook me awake and SCREAMED in my ear, "SOMETHING IS OUT THERE AND IT'S TRYING TO BREAK IN."

The year was 1990, and I worked in the log mill at Trader Cove, 25 miles north of Ketchikan. Cathy and I were living onboard a floating logging camp. Each of the houses was built four feet above a floating log platform. There were five, split-log steps leading to our back porch.

All summer long there was a channel of open water between each house, into which we could pull our boats. In winter, this channel would freeze solid and we would walk between the houses.

One midwinter night, Cathy was startled from a deep sleep by thrashing noises out on the back porch. Noises of such a contrast to the usual quiet surrounding us that she was panic stricken. Her body trembled as she violently shook me awake, all-the-while SCREAMING in my ear. *"SOMETHING IS OUT THERE AND IT'S TRYING TO BREAK IN."*

I bolted straight up and out of bed before my eyes opened and stumbled over my logging boots. As I jumped up in alarm, the cobwebs began to clear, and I was able to grasp the situation. Cathy was clearly shaken. I tried soothing her by explaining, "It's probably just one of the neighborhood dogs, sneaking up on our porch to steal my deer." That deer was our winter meat supply.

Still in my under shorts, I wiped a layer of frost from the kitchen window and peered out. What I saw startled me; it was a slow moving giant sausage-shape thing. The front end, the part that was reaching for the deer, tapered down to a small head with whiskers and small, beady eyes. The other end narrowed to a tail or flippers. Then it dawned on me–this monster salami was a sea lion.

He had slithered up the steps and onto my porch and was raising havoc, flopping around trying to reach my deer. This ruckus was just a few inches away from our back door, the door that didn't latch very well. That made me real nervous. All you had to do was bump this door and it would swing open into the house. I didn't want this big sea lion in my kitchen. To scare him off the porch, I opened the door and slammed it hard in his face. He didn't move. I opened the door a second time and slammed it harder. All he did was blink back at me. The third time I slammed the door, it didn't faze him at all. I told Cathy to calm down and get my .375 rifle before things got out of hand.

I cracked opened the window and yelled, "GET OUT OF HERE." His head was just below the window, and he looked up and seemed to smile; then he barked back at me. Man, talk about fish breath; it was awful. It was so bad, I felt my dinner rising back up in my throat. I swallowed hard, before firing several shots to scare him. He took the hint, and slipped back off my porch.

The sea lion had broken through the ice to come up onto our porch, and now he went out through a different hole in the ice. This second hole was near where I had a ¼-inch cable attached for my dog run. Cugo, my black lab was getting up in dog years. He was hard of hearing and would sleep in the house. Cugo's leash, still attached to the cable run, lay limp on the porch.

The sea lion got his tail flippers tangled up in the leash as he slid over the side. Off the porch he went, and through this second hole, with the leash on his flippers. With heavy springs on both ends, the cable erupted into bouncing, jerking motions. This ¼-inch cable was stretched near the breaking point several times in the few minutes before the sea lion worked itself free.

Neither Cathy nor I slept the rest of that night. At daybreak, I brought that deer in and as it thawed, I cut and wrapped each piece, filling our freezer until it bulged. I sure didn't want to leave anything outside that would lure that sea lion back for another visit.

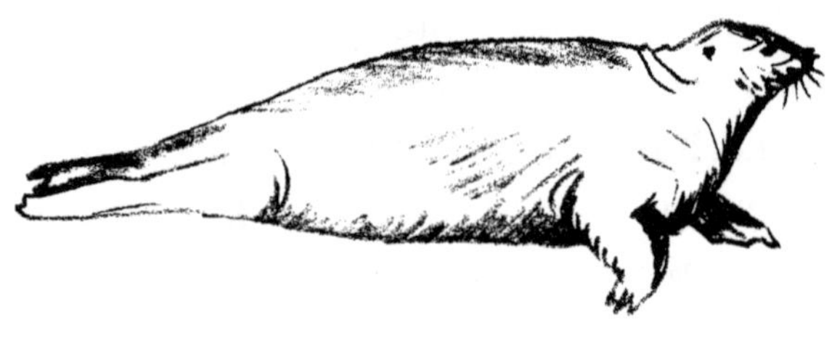

The Birds Were Falling Out Of the Trees

By Randy Moore

My wife was teaching school and I was trapping beaver in Rampart, a native village on the Yukon River. During the winter of 1988-89 a cold front moved in, and the temperature dropped to near 80° below zero. This deep freeze lasted for about a month.

It was so cold the small birds (Junco) were freezing and falling dead out of the trees. I wouldn't have believed it if I hadn't seen it with my own eyes.

They closed the school for four weeks because of the severe conditions. The town generator quit, and we needed a part or the whole village would be in deep trouble. Planes couldn't land because of snowdrifts on the runway, and our snowplows were frozen. We chartered a plane to fly over the airstrip and drop the part on the runway. That's how we were able to get the generator back on line.

We couldn't buy any gas because the pumps froze up down at the trading post. Our propane froze. The frost came right through the chinking between the logs of our cabin. The bed blankets froze to the outer wall. People can say that once it gets so cold, it doesn't really matter. That's not true. The colder it gets, the more things don't work.

Later I walked down the wide trail to the trading post, and a shrew came up out of his hole in the snow bank and started across the trail. The little varmint didn't make it; three quarters of the way across he went pegs up, froze to death right on the spot. I stood right there and watched him.

Many people in Rampart are lax about getting a good supply of firewood before winter. Now, when we were deep into the coldest weather, these families ran out of wood. You would hear a chainsaw fire up. Someone would run out of his house to the nearest tree, cut it down, saw it up, and run back in the house with it. When that tree was used up, he would fire up his chain saw again, run out of his house to the next closest tree, and cut it down. Come spring, Rampart didn't have many trees left in town.

- Sourdough Sam says-

"Alaska was the 49th state to join the Union and became part of the greatest Nation on earth, America. I'm real proud and thankful for that."

I've Seen the Alaska Few Outsiders See

By Diane Elbert

My heart skipped a beat in 1978 when, at age 17, I waited breathlessly in line with the other girls, trying to hold the same smile I had been holding since the judging first began. The MC opened the envelope and announced the winner. The new Miss Golden Heart of Fairbanks, Alaska is Miss Diane Elbert. Tears filled my eyes as I thanked everyone, and hugged the other girls. I will always remember that night.

As Miss Golden Heart, I was invited to travel to Nome, Barrow and St. Lawrence Island to perform in a children's TV program. I was able to experience my first dog sled ride, be tossed in an Eskimo blanket toss, and see an Alaska that few outsiders see. Upon landing on St. Lawrence Island, we were met by the entire village. They turned out on four wheelers and snowmobiles, all state-of-the-art vehicles. We went into one man's dark hut and watched him carve by hand the ivory treasures sold in expensive gift shops. That night we joined in an authentic Eskimo dance festival. In Barrow we saw the largest polar bear in captivity, and a whole captive wolf pack under observation.

In every village we visited, the houses were modest, but the state had provided a brand-new huge school, beautifully appointed and modern in all ways. This building served as the town center.

The spirit of these people was a true inspiration to me. They were living and doing without many of the conveniences I grew up with– running water, indoor plumbing, my own room. I was so thankful that my mom and dad had chosen to settle down in the big city of Fairbanks, instead of a remote village.

I Stood On Top of the World

By Jonathan & Susan Clark

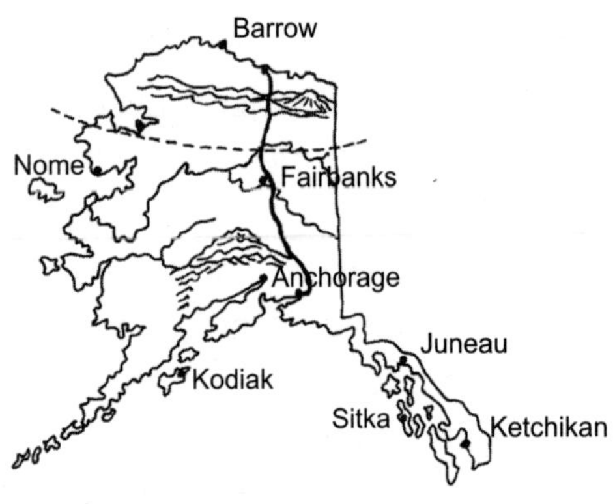

I've wanted to visit Barrow, Alaska ever since I was six years old. That's when I discovered the family atlas and proceeded to wear it out, as I learned everything I could about the world in which I lived. Not many kids just starting school know where the northernmost point on North America is. But I did, and getting to Point Barrow became a lifelong dream.

Now, at 43, I was achieving my dream. As our plane approached Barrow, the summer day was clear and the ice pack had just begun to break up on the coast. From the window, in the distance, I saw a small, curling spit of land north of town–Point Barrow.

Planning our visit to Barrow was exciting for Susan and me. We had several things on our "must-do" list: visit the place where Will Rogers and Wiley Post had crashed in 1935; take a series of pictures each hour, all through the night, of the never-setting sun as it crossed the northern sky; walk on the ice pack; and stand alone, further north than any human being on the North American continent, for a few minutes, at Point Barrow.

The ice pack was first. We marveled at the thickness of the ice, at the great mountains formed as it pushed up against the shore, at the small strip of the Arctic Ocean now visible as the pack began to recede for the short Arctic summer. I spent a sleepless night waking myself by alarm every 60 minutes, and taking a picture facing north from the Top of the World Hotel.

The next quest was Point Barrow, which is actually about eight miles from town, but only the first two miles had a road. The remaining six miles had to be negotiated in the thick, rocky gravel of the beach. We had already walked in it and experienced the "two steps forward, one step back" routine. The walk seemed difficult, if not impossible. So, we found a store that rented ATVs and we took out two of the three-wheel variety. We went for a practice run, and found that we had never driven vehicles so difficult to handle. When I wasn't turning mine over, I was running one of the big rear tires over the back of my leg as I tried to stop. We were bruised and bloodied, and gladly let the storeowner take them back and return our deposit.

Next, we stopped at a travel agency to inquire if there were any tours to Point Barrow. We had come so far, and we were determined. How could it be done? One of the women there told us that after her husband got off work they would get us in their four-wheeler. That's how we met Neil and Reeva Paskewitz. They only had one ATV, a four-wheeler, and it was one that an inexperienced person could handle. We went back and rented the three-wheelers again. Our new friends each rode a three-wheeler, and Susan and I sat together and navigated the four-wheeler.

We got to know Neil and Reeva on this outing. They had moved to Barrow from Minnesota, for jobs that paid five times more than the ones they left. Neil was a police officer, Reeva the city clerk. "He arrests them, and I book them," Reeva says.

We stopped on the way out to watch a native family coming off the ice pack, dragging a seal they had harpooned.

Finally we reached a small hilltop, and just ahead of us lay a curling spit of land extending into the Arctic Ocean. I stood on Point Barrow by myself for several minutes: the northernmost human being in North America.

The Grizzly Bear Was Up On His Hind Legs

By Paul Elbert

I looked up and there was this huge grizzly bear watching me.

It was the third morning of our moose hunt. Dick and I were camped in a secluded spot off the Savage River. We had hiked the hills and valleys the day before, and about wore my 63-year-old body out. Dick was younger and still had his get up and go, so he got up and prepared a hearty breakfast of bacon and eggs, and my homegrown potatoes. When we finished eating breakfast I went about 100 yards from camp down the narrow trail to the river, without my rifle, to wash the pot and frying pan. Somewhere between washing the pot and the fry pan, I heard a unfamiliar grunt. I looked up from my crouched position to see a full-grown grizzly bear not 40 feet from me across the shallow river. He was up on his hind legs, watching me. He must have smelled the bacon frying. I vigorously banged my pot and pan together and started yelling and shouting. That inquisitive big bear got down on all fours and turned and lumbered away. It took ten minutes before my quivering legs allowed me to walk on them and return to camp. The moral of this story is, "Don't leave your gun in camp."

Three Wolves Were Watching Me

By Bud Meyers

I heard rustling noises in the brush and had the eerie feeling...

It was late September, and I was camping out at my friend Adolph's cabin up near the mouth of the little Chena River. The sun had dropped behind the mountains, but the moon was out, shining bright on this clear night. I wanted to spear some whitefish for supper. I had seen several nice sized ones earlier in the day. I followed the narrow, winding trail 100 yards back to the river. I felt a little apprehensive when I heard rustling noises in the brush, but being a very macho guy I kept on walking. I thought it might be wolves, since there were tracks imbedded in the soft trail and droppings around. I continued on down to a large rock jutting out into the river, where I could see whitefish in the clear water.

I turned and looked back up the trail. There, in the middle of the trail, stood three wolves. They didn't howl or growl, they were just watching me, sizing me up. I began to get nervous when the largest gray wolf eased several steps in my direction. I didn't have a gun for protection, just my three-prong fish spear, and I couldn't attack them with just one spear. I knew I couldn't outrun them. All I could do was stand and watch them watching me. I stood there about twenty minutes in this stare-down. Their big, round, yellow, marble-looking eyes never even blinked. I didn't want to spend the night on the riverbank, so I figured I might as well take a chance and try to bluff them. Swallowing my fear, I glared back at them, and started walking with conviction in their direction. I could see the hair rising on the back of their necks as I approached. The two smaller wolves moved to the side leaving the large wolf in front, but I just kept coming.

I used to box and remembered the fear I often felt before a big fight. The feeling of staring across the ring at a big strapping guy whose every intention was to knock me out. The empty, all-alone, ready-to-fight for my life feeling that I had now was worse than before any of my big fights, but I kept walking, waving my spear, glaring, and bluffing.

The moment of truth arrived as I got close, where something was going to happen. Now, with just 20 feet between us, the wolves turned in unison and slinked off into the underbrush. I could breathe again. The confrontation was over, but I lost any desire for whitefish, or even supper.

I Took My Sons Hunting

By Don Elbert

We were lost, and the mosquitoes were eating us alive.

My sons Dave and Ken, 15 and 12 years old, and I were off bonding. I took my boys moose hunting by riverboat across the Tanana River and up Clear Creek, 45 miles from town. We hunted the river for moose morning and night, and mixed in duck hunting, fishing for grayling and talking in the daytime. The sun was high overhead on the third day, as we followed a flock of ducks that flew just a ways off the river, and seemed to land. Thinking that there was a lake just off the river, we went after them. After about 25 minutes of walking, sometimes crawling through the thick under-brush, around willows and falling in muskeg (tundra), all the while slapping those bloodsucking mosquitoes, we stopped. With no sign of a lake in sight I told my boys, "Let's turn back. I don't want to get lost in here."

I looked around for some sign or direction to get back to the river, but couldn't see any landmark from where we were. From inside the thick brush all we could see is more brush. The sun was still overhead, so that was no help; we were disoriented. We started to walk back, but I really didn't have a clue what direction to take. I told my boys that we were in trouble, and that this could be very serious. I didn't want to alarm them, but figured they should know our situation. Dave's face took on a cold, blank stare, and I noticed tears welling up in Ken's eyes, as they grew increasingly sad. I said, "Okay, you two are in the Scouts, what direction do you think the river is?"

Dave's voice wavered as he pointed and said, "Dad, I

think we came from over that way."

So we started out in that direction, and again attempted to find the easiest way through the brush and in and around the thick clumps of scraggly willows. The mosquitoes were on us like stink on a six-week-old decayed moose carcass. Smashing mosquitoes became our primary means of surviving, as they were attempting to siphon our life's blood.

We kept moving, and the minutes ticked by as I began visualizing all the fatal things that could happen if we didn't find our way back to the creek. Like being eaten alive by mosquitoes, becoming bear bait, starvation, exposure. If, in fact, we were walking away from the river, we never would be found. I thought about my wife, Elaine, and the pain that she would go through if the boys and I didn't return. And our dream house that she designed-it wouldn't be built. I thought about our daughter, Diane, and our younger boys, Karl and Doug, growing up without a father. "Oh God," I prayed out loud, "Don't let us die out here like this. Please, God, give us one chance–I won't walk away from the river again." I felt sick inside, helpless, and at the mercy of the sometimes-cruel Mother Nature.

We had walked endlessly for three hours, when I heard a trickle of water off to my right. The first glimpse of hope and direction surfaced, as we turned and walked toward that trickle. The welcome sound of running water grew louder, as we scurried the 100 yards and burst out on the bank of Clear Creek. We were four miles upstream from my boat. The overpowering feeling of relief from this heaviest load of worries that was crushing me, flooded every cell of my being and brought immediate tears to my eyes. Unconsciously, I reached for my boys and hugged them tight for several minutes before Ken spoke up. "Let's go home, Dad!"

I agreed. At that moment, nothing in the world was more important than going home. With this thought in mind, our steps and our spirits were much livelier than they had been in the last three hours. We made it back to the boat in record time; made a quick stop at camp, took down the tent, loaded our gear, and headed home.

Once we reached the Tanana River, I looked over at my sons, Dave and Ken, my emotions exploded and tears of joy flowed. From my head and my heart I felt a much stronger and renewed love and kinship toward my boys. I believe we had truly bonded.

-Machismo can get you frozen-
Respect Mother Nature for she is a worthy adversary.

My first trip hooked me on Alaska

By Bill Griffin

I'd read and heard a lot about Alaska, back in the mid-fifties and I wanted to go, but deep inside I never believed I would. Driving the highway was a real problem back then, and I had a wife and six kids and a job. There was no way I would ever get to Alaska.

Then one day my brother called. Now my brother is the most adventurous guy I've ever seen, and in my opinion he is probably the world's best bush pilot. My brother came to Alaska earlier and was working as a mechanical engineer when they built the Clear Air Force Base. At the end of that job he bought some airplanes and started an air taxi operation called Clear Air Taxi, at Clear, Alaska.

He called me and said, "Why don't you come up here to Alaska and go hunting with me?" Boy, I thought that was really great. So I took my two-week vacation from my job. I booked a flight on Pan American and flew to Alaska. He met me at the airport in Fairbanks and we had a grand reunion. Next morning I obtained my hunting license etc. and my brother promptly loaded me and his hunting partner Jim, in his

Cessna 180. He flew us straight up in the Brooks Range.

So there I was, fresh out of the big city, where there are people everywhere you look. Now I'm flying over this vast country with no one around for hundreds of miles. I was impressed. I just knew this was my kind of country.

We started flying between those mountain peaks and I said to my brother, "now, what do you do if your engine quits?" He said, "you don't think about that." But you can't help think about that, because there's no place to land. If your engines quit you're gonna crash your airplane, and worry about not getting killed yourself. We spotted some rams on the side of the mountain. We landed safely on a short gravel bar up in the Brooks Range and made camp. In the morning the three of us walked about five miles to get to the mountain. We climbed up where the sheep were and they weren't there. We discovered we were on the wrong mountain and had to come back down. I wasn't in such good shape either and I was feeling it already.

But, we knew the sheep were on one of those mountains so we started climbing the next mountain. In places it seemed to be almost straight up. In places there were bushes growing, I'd grab the bushes to steady myself and help pull me up. With a pack on my back, combined with a tired body and a sore gut, climbing that mountain was a tremendous job! We got up on a high ridge of that mountain about 1:00 PM. That's where we'd seen the sheep, but they weren't there. We were all so tired and beat, we lay down and went to sleep. It was September and the sun was shining warmly.

I woke first and I just walked over a little ridge, not far, and there they were, the sheep, right there. Two nice full-curl rams stood out. Boy, was I excited. All the time we'd been sleeping, those rams were just over the ridge. I hurried back, awakened the guys, and we cautiously returned. I shot the biggest ram, and the other one took off and Jim shot him. We had two big full-curl rams. By now it's along about 4:00 PM, and it would be dark before long. Now we faced the problem of getting the meat and the heads down this mountain. It was real work. We packed all the meat we could carry out on the first trip. I got the head of my sheep, with the hide attached, and put that on my head and it was heavy. Jim had his sheep head on his head also, and my brother had all the meat he could carry. Then we started down, and hoping to save time we took a shortcut. This turned out to be a very bad idea.

We went down, down, and after about an hour of climbing down we finally got to this cliff that dropped straight down. We couldn't carry our sheep heads down. It was all we could do to clutch with our hands to get down there without falling forty feet. So we took these heads and the meat and let them down with a rope. Jim climbed down there, and my brother lowered our packs down by a rope. The guy down below untied the rope and my brother pulled it back up. This is the way we got all the sheep and gear, down the cliff, and then we climbed down. And we walked about another half a mile and got to an impossible spot where it was just a cliff going down hundreds of feet, no way out. Couldn't make it, can't get out. We had to go back to this place where we had lowered everything down by the rope and had to do it in reverse. My brother climbed up, secured the rope, and pulled our stuff back up. By the time he got everything back up, night had fallen and it was dark. There we were carrying this fresh sheep meat; blood smeared on us and with signs of grizzly bears all over the place. We'd seen one grizzly coming in; bear tracks and droppings were everywhere. We were extremely nervous and ill at ease. On top of that I was hurting and my muscles ached. Anyway, we finally made it down, right down to the Dietrich River. My brother and his friend just ran off and left me. They were hunters and in better shape.

I was all by myself, walking with my sheep head on my back; I didn't stop to dwell on what a danger that was. I got so tired I'd sit down and rest, then up again, walk and walk. We had gone about six miles up there. I got to a river and I had to cross it and I didn't want to get my boots wet. So I sat down and took my boots off. I threw one across, about forty feet to the sand and the gravel on the other side, and I started to throw my second boot across-oops, it slipped, I was so weak, it hit right in the middle of the river and sunk. Now here I was, a sheep head on my back, carrying my gun, dead tired, one boot in about probably two or three feet of water, the other boot on the other bank. So I waded out in that ice cold water. I found my boot and threw it on the bank. Went back and got my sheep and my gun, waded the river again, put my boots on, disgusted, got my sheep head and finally made it back to camp.

The next morning, I tried to stand--but fell. I couldn't even get up without help. My legs didn't move and my knees wouldn't bend but my head and my heart had adopted this great country.

I Caught a 254-Pound Halibut

By Wiley Harris

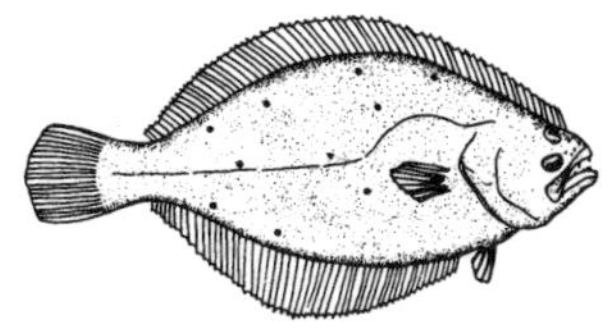

It was big, almost twice as much as I weigh. I was so proud, that I had the tail mounted.

Few experiences in life come close to matching the thrill I felt in 1986, when I brought up that whale of a halibut. The sun was squinting through scattered clouds that morning as our charter boat departed Halibut Cove, in Kachemak Bay. We traveled around 35 mph for three hours over calm water, before stopping and dropping anchor. Five men and two women made up our group, each wanting to catch a big one. We baited our hooks with herring, dropped them overboard, and waited. An older lady caught the first small halibut, and then her husband brought up a 25 pound'er. In the first few hours, everyone had caught at least one, except me. Then it happened, I hooked into something and my fishing pole nearly bent double. I thought it was a sunken vessel or maybe the bottom of the ocean. The captain had everyone else reel in, so as not to tangle with my line. I reeled and reeled. It was a dead weight; there was no fight at all. I got worn out reeling. I only weigh 135 pounds. The captain had to help me reel in whatever I had. An hour later, up comes this huge, flat halibut, then it wakes up mad and starts to fight. Our captain shot the halibut and gaffed it, so that we could bring it aboard. It was big, almost twice as much as I weigh. I was so proud, that I had the tail mounted and it now hangs on my wall. I relive that special moment everytime I look up at that tail and envision how big he looked laid out on deck.

Gold Nuggets

By Karl Mock

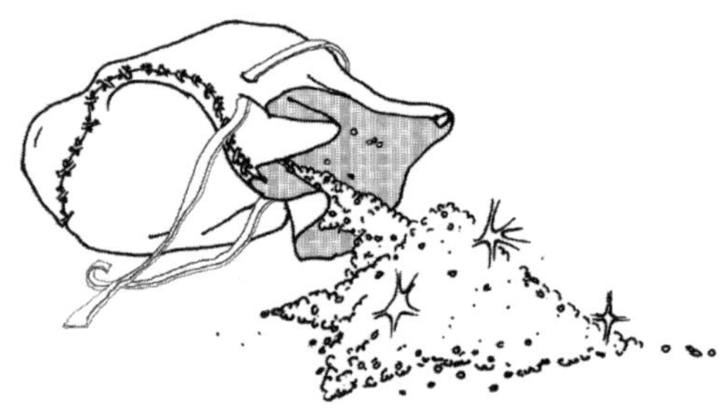

The sign read, "Do Not Pick Up Any Gold Nuggets in the Tailing Piles."

I worked on the gold dredge in Ester for the Fairbanks Exploration Company back in the early days of gold dredging. The tourists and the local folks used to come out to Ester, climb up on the tailing piles for a closer look, and watch the gold dredge in operation. We had to put up a fence for their safety so they wouldn't get too close. We also put up several big signs warning the people not to pick up any gold nuggets they might see in the tailings.

For a little added excitement another crewmember and I, in our spare time, used to melt brass welding rod into what looked like shiny gold nuggets. Then on occasion before work we would strategically scatter these nuggets around inside the fenced area. Surreptitiously, we would watch the people out of the corner of our eye while we worked on the dredge. When we would spot someone overcome with temptation, bend over and pretend to scratch a leg or tie a shoe, and then pick up one of these authentic-looking nuggets, we would blow the whistle and hoot and holler and wave. People got the strangest expression on their face when caught red-handed.

The Fleas Took Over our Cabin

By Beverly Kersey

During our second year in Alaska, my husband and I made an effort to really get a feel of this country. We ran a ten-mile trap line. We had a cabin on the Chatanika River and a snowmobile, so we bought a box of traps and set them on the trail to our cabin. We caught mostly fox and one wolverine. We would bring the frozen animals back home to thaw out so we could skin them and prepare the hide to stretch and dry. But once the animals started to thaw, we both started scratching and itching like crazy. We discovered they had fleas, and the fleas came to life in the warm house environment, and would leave the cold corpses they were on to land on our warm bodies and start drilling for blood. They were so thick, the ones that weren't on us you could see flying around the room.

We rushed into town in a desperate attempt to buy some Raid to kill the fleas. However, this was the middle of winter and stores do not stock or sell many cans of Raid in the winter. We were able to find a few cans in the basement of the Co-op Drug store and went home and thoroughly sprayed the house in a desperate attempt to reclaim it from the fleas.

My exposed skin looked like rough sandpaper from all the bumps that erupted from bites.

Winter on the Edge of the Bering Sea

By Father Gerald Ornowski

Grit and humor live side by side; beauty and tragedy are bedfellows. That's life in Eskimo Alaska.

She was bent over, head low, hands resting on her knees, face almost touching the snow. Resting. Many of the old Eskimos do it that way. The 76- year-old had been trudging through the deep snow on her way home from visiting a friend at the far end of the village. Against the crisp cold of the December day she was clad in sealskin mukluks and fur parka, which she had made.

I came along on my snowmachine, checking out the new track I had installed. We had just endured a three-day storm, our first big snow of the winter that had piled up drifts five feet high. I wanted to make sure my machine was fit for the months of hard riding that lay ahead.

I call her by her Eskimo name, Manchoan, although somewhere along the way she had picked up the English name, Alice. Throughout Eskimoland, teachers and government agents used to replace Eskimo names with more familiar ones like Joe, Pete, and Mary. Some trading post managers even gave the names of commodities. Thus we have Eskimos whose last name are Coffee, Tea, Beans, Sugar, not to mention Sundown, Cowboy and Snowball.

Manchoan was still panting when I roared up. She doesn't speak English and I don't speak Yup'ik, but a few gestures made it clear that I was offering her a ride. Laboriously, a buxom Manchoan climbed on behind. It was then that I realized that a huge drift stood directly in front of us. I didn't want to ask her to get off again, so I decided to gun the motor to launch us over the drift. I hit the throttle hard and-varrumm!-we lurched ahead. Snow sprayed into the air as we hit the drift and hurtled over! But something was funny; I couldn't feel anyone behind. I glanced back and there was no Manchoan in sight. I ran back to the drift. There she was on the other side, sprawled in the snow, uttering words unintelligible. I knelt down in the snow beside her, checking for injuries. Nothing. Then with apology in my eyes, I looked into her face and we both began to laugh our heads off.

That's life in Eskimo Alaska. Grit and humor live side by side; beauty and tragedy are bedfellows. To this day, I can bring a broad smile to Manchoan's face whenever I say: "Me, you, Ski-doo!"

I came to the villages of St. Michael and Stebbins just over a year ago, the first priest of the Marians of the Immaculate Conception to work in Alaska. One of our specialties is to go where the need is greatest and the church's work is most neglected. I had helped in Western Alaska previously for short periods of time, relieving priests in the bush while they went "Outside" for retreat, vacation, and check-up. But this was to be my first full-blown winter. And "full-blown" is the word!

St. Michael and Stebbins are located on the shore of the Bering Sea, 500 miles from any road system, and from cities like Anchorage and Fairbanks. The Arctic wind comes howling unabated across the sea from Siberia. As I travel between the villages by snowmobile in winter and ATV in summer, the rain and the snow often slash against my face at 50 miles an hour. With winter temperatures at 30-to-40 degrees below zero, the windchill plunges to minus 80-to-100. Our link to the broader world-small bush planes that bring mail and supplies-don't fly in such weather. But I haven't missed a Sunday-celebrating Liturgy at one village in the morning, then scurrying ten miles across the tundra to the other village for celebration in the evening. It can be tough, even dangerous. Some years ago the Jesuit Superior issued a special warning about the windstorms between St. Michael and Stebbins. Some of my predecessors had suffered severe frostbite, and one Jesuit Brother froze to death near Stebbins, when a storm obscured the trail. I've suffered a little frostbite, and a lot of inconvenience, but the closest I've come to tragedy was the time I tried a different winter trail and missed Stebbins by two miles. The winter darkness lifted enough that I could spot the bluff above the village, and was able to follow the shoreline safely there.

But not all is gloom and doom; even the coldest, darkest winter has its moments of beauty. I remember two in particular: Christmas and potlatch.

Christmas 1990 came quickly. I had just become acquainted with the two villages, secured winter supplies, patched leaks and cracks on the buildings and was adjusting to the lengthening darkness (about 22 hours in mid-December), when it was time to begin my Christmas visits. I had decided to visit every household in the two villages with a card, a personal greeting, and the schedule of church services. It was a winning tactic for the "new Father," because most Eskimos feel honored to have a priest visit their house, no matter how poor and crowded it may be. And I got to know my people better.

Then came the decoration of the churches. No real trees, of course, in a land of treeless tundra, but I found plenty of lights and ornaments and a Nativity set with its share of broken ears and noses. Volunteers, especially the children, came forth to do the job.

Midnight Mass is a big thing; even the seldom-seen show up. I couldn't have it in both churches, so Stebbins got the nod this year. It featured wall-to-wall people and the hearty singing of Christmas hymns in Yup'ik. I felt a thrill run through me as I walked down the aisle holding aloft the figure of the Baby Jesus, placing it in the manger as we sang "O Holy Night." This is why I had come here, to bring God to these people. As young and old came forward to reverence the scene, I prayed that God-come-to-earth would shed the light of His truth and the warmth of His love on this cold, dark corner of the world.

Another Mass at noon on Christmas day helped accommodate the 400 inhabitants of the village. Then across the tundra to St. Michael for evening Mass, and much the same there. Because of traveling, I missed the celebration at the community hall when Santa arrives and gives goodies to kids of all ages.

A final vivid memory of Christmas Eve: colored lights in people's windows glistening on mounds of snow outside, and the aroma of driftwood smoke wafting into the air from the chimneys of little houses. We even had caroling. A group of school children came to sing–in English, with a Yup'ik accent.

All in all a memorable Christmas, including phone calls (via satellite) to the Marians in Massachusetts and to my mom in Michigan.

The other reprieve from the rigor of winter is potlatch–a long weekend of Eskimo dancing and feasting. It comes in March, when the darkness has lifted but the ice-clamp of winter is still heavy upon us. Activity has been restricted; some people are going crazy with cabin fever.

For weeks ahead, the singers and dancers have been practicing. Songs are composed about village life, and with stylized gestures telling the story, danced to the beat of drums. It's also a time to welcome visitors from other villages with plenty of food and conversation.

I had to be absent when Stebbins celebrated its potlatch, but a few weeks later the folks prevailed upon me to go with them to the potlatch in Kotlik, a neighboring village about 70 miles down the coast by snowmobile. Have you ever ridden a bucking bronco for 70 miles? Fierce winds had driven waves of snow across the trail, turning it into a frozen washboard. The jarring ride jangled all my bones and withered the strength in my arms.

But that's not all. Less than halfway there, my motor erupted into loud explosions and sputtered to a halt. What!? In vain I pulled the rope and worked the throttle to get it going. Wow! Breakdown on the Bering Sea. I stopped for a moment and surveyed my situation. The sea ice and drifts of snow stretched endlessly to the horizon. I felt like a BB on a hockey rink.

Fortunately, I hadn't tried this trip alone. I was following the tracks of a parishioner who shortly noticed that I had dropped behind. He circled back, then diagnosed my problem as a blown piston. I had two cylinders; could I make it on one or should we abandon the machine until a later time? Nope, a storm could prevent our retrieving it for a long time. (A storm actually did come up!) I chose to purr along slowly on one cylinder; he patiently followed behind. We made it to Kotlik and later back home again.

The potlatch was a neat experience: food, fun, new folks and the invitation to invoke God's blessing on each evening's celebration. I renewed acquaintance with Fr. Henry Hargreaves, S.J., the priest who covers the string of villages next to mine. Nevertheless, it is probably that breakdown on the trail that I remember most.

It took 26 days before I received through the mail all the parts necessary to replace that piston. That's a part of life here, too. The limited supplies carried by one or two village stores necessitates ordering things by catalog and telephone, then waiting for the barge or the plane to bring them. Frozen out of my house in St. Michael for eight days once when the furnace broke down, I stayed with one of the schoolteachers while waiting for parts. And while waiting for that snowmobile piston I had to beg rides-during the busy time of Holy Week, no less. But my vulnerability actually drew me closer to some of the men who don't often make it to church. Blessings in disguise!

That's a brief glimpse of winter life on the coast of the Bering Sea. The heart of the story here is not the struggle with the elements, albeit that's ever present. The real adventure is preaching God's word, touching hearts, relieving pain, walking the journey. The weather, isolation, and the unfamiliar culture just increase the challenge. For the younger generation of Eskimos the impact of White culture, coming primarily via the schools and the media (satellite TV), has added confusion and frustration to an already tough life. I cannot turn back the sweep of time and technology, or the new social patterns that uproot the old ones. But I can stand at people's sides during a painful moment in their history; I can point to something besides sex and alcohol as a way out of pain. I can offer the healing love of a God whose light and strength transcend cultural boundaries.

In our struggle together I constantly find "flowers on the tundra," even in the midst of winter: the faithful few who come to every church service I have; the lady who translates for me to the old folks; the man who has worked on my snowmachine three times; the folks who bring homemade bread and fish and berries; the disconsolate husband whose wife left him with three kids and no job, who deposited his gun with me so he wouldn't do something drastic; the old fellow who doesn't understand English but shakes both my hands after Mass; the fellow who exclaimed, "I never heard such wonderful things about God!"

Those things serve to lighten the burden, warm the frigid days, and speed me along the trail. Sometimes I dream for things, especially more helpers and an airplane. I could extend my ministry. But God will set the pace and provide the wherewithal. My job is to be faithful.

Whaling In The Arctic

By George Hotrum

Whaling in the Arctic is an ancient and dangerous art. To the Eskimos who live along the Arctic coast of Alaska, whaling is not a sport but a serious business. To their ancestors, not catching a whale could mean starvation.

Our umiak (Eskimo skin boat) moved silently through the Arctic water as we swiftly approached our quarry, a 50-foot bowhead whale. Sproosh, sproosh, the spouting of the whale became louder and louder as we closed the distance. The crew moved the umiak into position for the kill, inches from the whale's head as the gunner took careful aim with the ancient brass bomb gun. A misplaced shot could bring a mountain of enraged black muscle thrashing down upon the crew.

The gunner signaled that he was ready. The crew carefully edged the umiak forward upon the neck of the submerged whale. BOOM! The ancient gun fired, driving the projectile deep into the neck. Our umiak was lifted high out of the water upon the flailing fins as the whale dove. Then everything was calm as the whale disappeared into the depths of the ocean.

Anxious looks were exchanged among the crew. Is the whale dead? Is he trapped beneath the ice? Will he surface? These questions and many more ran through our minds as we silently prayed and waited. Losing a 50-ton whale would be a severe loss to the village of Point Barrow. The Natives depend upon the muktuk and whale meat to fill their ice cellars for the coming year.

The water was cloudy, which made it difficult to see the slowly emerging shape of the dying giant. Cheers of victory filled the arctic air, as the motionless mammal floated to the surface.

We harpooned the whale and attached floats to keep it from sinking until we could pull it up onto the ice. One of the proud crew members placed a flag high upon an ice ridge as a signal to other crews: Come quickly! We need help!

Whaling in the Arctic is an ancient and dangerous art. To the Eskimos who live along the Arctic coast of Alaska, whaling is not a sport but a serious business. To their ancestors, not catching a whale could mean starvation. But this is no longer true today. Many of the villagers are employed by oil companies or have other well-paying jobs. They live in modern, frame houses–many with indoor plumbing and have color TVs.

Point Barrow, a village of about 2,500 people located at the top of the world, is the largest of the Eskimo villages. It is the farthest-north point on the North American continent. It boasts a new $1.5 million hotel, a restaurant, three taxicabs, a large store, and an airport with jet service. However, the old ways of the ancestors, whaling in particular, still persist.

Spring whaling in Barrow begins each year around the last week in April. Temperatures have risen enough, -10° to +10°, to cause the Arctic ice pack to begin to move, opening leads of water for the whales to pass through. A lead is a wide channel of water that has opened in the ice because of the pressure of the ice pack and the Arctic winds.

The men load their wooden freight sleds, pulling them across the ice with their Sno-gos in search of a good lead. There they make camp, and wait for a whale. The umiak is placed at the edge of the ice, ready for a quick launch.

The umiak is a wood-framed boat usually about sixteen feet long and covered with handsewn ugruk-bearded sealskins. The umiak makes no noise when it is pushed from the ice, and if it strikes a jagged piece of ice while in pursuit of a whale or while trying to escape the attack of an enraged 2,000-pound walrus, the tough skin will bounce off the ice. An aluminum or fiberglass boat is too noisy, and would sink if it struck a sharp piece of ice. You can survive for only a few minutes in the frigid waters of the Arctic.

When a whale is sighted swimming down the lead, the crew quickly launches the umiak and begins pursuit. They delicately man the wooden paddles as the gunner or harpooner of the crew awaits the right moment, for a misplaced shot could mean a lost whale or, worse yet, drowning to the crew.

The ancient whale gun is made of solid brass and weighs about 30 pounds. Dating back to the 1800s, it is not very efficient, but it is the best equipment available. Quite often the gun misfires and the whale has to be harpooned by hand.

The crew approaches the whale from the side, behind the eye so that they will not be detected. They paddle the umiak up on the whale's neck and the gunner fires into the neck-joint. If placed properly, the shot breaks the neck and the whale is unable to dive. Sometimes the whale gets caught under the ice and is lost. When the whale surfaces, harpoons with floats attached are embedded into the whale to keep it afloat or to slow its flight, if only wounded.

Word of the catch is sent back to the village, and everyone available turns out to help. A whale weighs one ton per foot in length, so it takes a lot of help to pull a 50-ton giant from the water. Sometimes the ice has to be blasted out with dynamite to create a channel so that the whale can be pulled to ice solid enough to support its tremendous weight.

Anchor rods are driven into the ice. One end of a block and tackle is attached to the rods and the other end to the whale by a large band. It may take 100 people two or three days to pull a large whale far enough onto the ice so cutting can begin.

Large knives on long poles called "flensing knives" are used to peel muktuk from the carcass. The muktuk is thick whale skin and blubber about 18 inches thick. It is quite tasty, resembling the flavor of sardines. Under the muktuk is the rich red meat of the whale.

The baleen (or whale's gums), which filters the microscopic organisms from the water for food, is used for Eskimo art. It is polished to a high black sheen suitable for etching, or torn into strips and woven into baskets.

The inner ear of the whale, which is a bone about 10 inches in diameter, is the most prized possession, and is always given to the captain of the crew.

The whale meat and blubber are cut into strips and hauled by sled into the village, then stored in underground ice cellars. These ice cellars have been dug into the permafrost and keep meat frozen year round. After whaling season, the Eskimos hold a festival with everyone participating in playing games and eating muktuk.

Every Thanksgiving a feast is held at the church. Those who caught a whale share with everyone who did not. A generous, equal portion of muktuk and whale meat is passed out to children and adults alike. It is a true Thanksgiving feast in the real meaning and tradition of Thanksgiving.

Why do the men work so hard and risk so much? Is it because of their ancestors? Tradition? Economics? I don't know if anyone really knows for sure. One man who left a high-paying job on the North Slope to come home for whaling explained, "I like fresh whale meat."

Up here at the top of the world we all do, which I suppose is a good part of what whaling is all about.

-Animal life in the wild, is not kind -

It's an animal eat animal world out there and the bears and the whales are at the top of their respected food chain.

Josephine the Friendly Moose

By Paul Angelo Elbert

Few families are so fortunate as to have a wild creature for a pet. Of those, even fewer have the patience and gentleness to win the trust of such a creature. But when such a relationship does exist, it is one that brings out all that is best and most admirable in that family. This is the story of just such a family.

Every year moose came to the Dolney homestead near Fairbanks, to eat from the large garden. The first meeting of the moose and the Dolneys came one evening in late October of 1965. Shep, the collie dog, announced the arrival of a cow and calf moose, who began feeding at the far end of the garden. They pawed up, and ate the coarse cabbage leaves, kale, and broccoli stalks. They ate their fill and left.

On succeeding evenings Shep's sharp and distinctive bark came only briefly, as a signal to the Dolneys that the moose had returned for another meal.

Now the garden was large, an acre or more. As the moose ate their fill each evening and depleted the far end of the garden, they edged nearer and nearer to the house. Finally, all that remained were the frozen, dried-up sweet pea vines that clung to trellises beside the house. When the moose began eating these, the Dolneys–five in all, Ed, Ann, Linda, Karen and Walter–peered excitedly through the thermopane window. Never had two moose come so close before.

The next night the cow and the calf came back to finish the remaining vines. Those gone, they looked around for something more. The calf was fearless. It sauntered over to the back porch, attracted by the carrots, potato peelings, and cabbage leaves in the yellow garbage pail. The mother moose followed. Since her calf had preempted the pail of peelings, she looked enviously at Shep's supper. The pancakes and bread crusts were to her liking. As she munched them, she seemed to smack her lips. Selfishly, she butted her calf away when it tried to join her.

Ann, wishing to continue these exciting moose visits, spread out two loaves of bread over the back porch the next night. One loaf was for the cow, and one for the calf. But the cow wanted it all for herself, so she chased her calf around the house. This was fun and exciting for the Dolneys as they rushed from one window to the next to watch. Ann continued the feeding in the days that followed, buying stale bread at the Fairbanks bakeries.

The moose loved it, and they ate every crumb. They robbed the bird feeder and knocked it over several times. It was set aside, far back on the porch. The snow birds, jays and squirrels had lost out to a far more interesting pet.

One night the cow moose chased her calf away from the bread again. Ann's heart went out to the calf. She picked up a loaf of bread and stepped out the side door. Ed and the children watched breathlessly. Was it safe to get so close to a calf moose? What would the mother do?

Ann held out a slice of bread. Her heart pounded as the calf came to her. It was tall and awkward. With feminine determination, Ann steeled herself for the encounter, whatever it might be. Without hesitation the calf came, gentle as a Jersey cow.

Slice after slice, she ate the loaf of bread from Ann's hands. Soft as a kiss, her lips touched Ann's fingers. The bread gone, Ann slipped back into the house, wide-eyed at her feat of daring. The family looked at her incredulously. She had done something very special. She had been accepted as a benefactor and friend by the calf. She had captured its trust and confidence.

The children clamored to get into the act. Soon, they too were feeding the calf, the mother standing back a little. First Karen, then Linda, and finally little Walter, fed the moose. The gentleness of the little moose was a revelation of adaptability.

One day a box of stale bread was set far back on the porch, out of the reach of either moose. The little calf thought to climb the porch and get it. She put her front feet onto the slick fiberglass covering, and fell on her tummy, long legs spread out in every direction. Finally she rolled back, fell off the porch and scrambled to her feet. After that, neither moose ever attempted to get onto the porch again.

The keen edge of excitement and high adventure was beginning to dull by the time spring arrived. Many pictures had been taken, hundreds of loaves of bread had been consumed.

The cow moose was heavy with another calf. In mid-April she slipped off quietly to her nursery in one of the lush, nearby swamps. She weaned last year's calf, leaving it to the tender care of the Dolneys.

After considerable discussion, the family decided that the calf should be named. And assuming it to be of masculine gender, they named it Joe. But one day, in the front yard they realized that they had made a mistake, and that Joe was a she. So the name was lengthened to the more appropriate Josephine, and then to Jo, for short.

In mid-May Ann was busy seeding vegetables and flowers, and transplanting the thousands of plants that had been started in the greenhouse. The leaves were turning green, and Ed and Ann decided that it was time to quit feeding Jo.

At noon Ann looked out her kitchen window and saw Josephine's big hungry mouth menacingly near some valuable plants. Ann exploded out the kitchen door, shouting "No, no, Jo!" Rather than flee, Josephine came to Ann, refusing to believe that Ann was trying to get rid of her. There was a hurt look in her eye. Ann wiped the blanket of mosquitoes off Jo's nose and from around her eyes.

Then Ann talked to Josephine again, and Josephine listened. She apparently understood that the garden plants were not for her just then. She walked out of the driveway, crossed the road and disappeared into the brush beyond. She would leave Ann's garden alone, and let her raise and sell her vegetables and flowers unmolested.

In summer, Shep's job was to keep the big, hungry snowshoe hares away from the garden, while the Maltese cat, and a red fox kept the field mice under control. The garden thrived. Kale and broccoli grew tall, and several cabbages reached 30 pounds in weight. Flowers bloomed in such profusion, that the front yard looked like a rainbow.

Autumn came and the vegetables were harvested and

stored. Much refuse remained on the ground, such as culled carrots, turnips, potatoes, beets and radishes, as well as the big, coarse, outer leaves of cabbage and cauliflower, and the big kale and broccoli stalks.

October snows came and stayed. The time was approaching when wild moose would come and feast on what was left of the garden. But could wild beasts remember? Would Josephine or her mother return? The Dolneys did hope ardently that their moose would return. It was not until November that Shep gave his sharp moose bark. The Dolney family rushed to the windows. There was indeed a cow moose and her calf in the far end of the garden, nonchalantly eating, even as Josephine and her mother had done the fall before. These moose were not afraid of Shep. But was it Josephine's mother? Was the adventure of the previous fall about to be re-enacted? The Dolneys were delighted and their hopes were high, but they were due for disappointment. The cow and her calf fed for a month straight, and then for some unknown reason stopped coming. It was not Josephine's mother, or else she had completely forgotten their friendship.

A long, lonesome month passed, and the Dolneys kept hoping that Josephine or her mother would return. December 14th arrived and Ann had just taken two still-steaming, blueberry pies out of the oven to cool. She glanced up at the kitchen clock, which read 3:30. Sudden movement, something outside the window, caught her attention. Like a returning angel, Josephine waltzed down the driveway, up to the porch, and expectantly stood there.

The prodigal calf had returned to be fed. Ann had two packages of hamburger buns, and fed them to Josephine one at a time. When the children came home, Josephine again allowed her nose to be petted and kissed. Joyfully, Ann resumed the procuring of stale bread from the bakeries, and vegetable trim from the grocery stores. Josephine loved every mouthful, every caress, every kiss, and every kind word. It was, in truth, a mutual admiration society.

A week later, Josephine's mother returned without a calf. Several times she came to the porch and ate with Josephine, but she seemed timid and ill at ease. Finally, she stopped coming. Josephine did not seem to notice, or mind her mother's departure. She had been weaned the previous spring, and now was entirely on her own. She must fend for herself or perish.

Josephine now had the Dolney family all to herself, as well as the feed, and she proceeded to utilize all. The moose was now a year and a half old, weighed a good 600 pounds, and stood six feet tall at the shoulders. Her appetite was enormous. She ate a box of vegetable trim and six-to-eight loaves of bread for a meal. Some days she came for all three meals.

The appetite of the Paul Bunyan-sized pet would have stopped most homesteaders from feeding her, but not the Dolneys. To Ann, the gathering of stale bread and vegetable trim was a labor of love. She was trusted, and she would not fail. The children were just as considerate and devoted.

Most moose are awkward, but Josephine walked down the drive on her four feet and stilt-like legs with the precision of a ballet dancer. She stepped over trikes, bikes and toys and never damaged a thing.

Josephine loved her adopted home so much that she would often stand for hours after feeding, looking in one or the other window, her breath on the glass. She would then reverse her stance for a while, and face the highway like a sentinel on guard. Then, maybe she would paw in the garden or browse on the birch trees in the yard.

One morning Josephine took over Shep's job of escorting Karen and Linda to the school bus. Her big body blocked the road, and the bus driver was obliged to sound his horn long and loud. Josephine promptly and politely stepped aside.

On March 10, 1967, disappointment struck: Josephine stopped coming. The Dolneys feared the worst. Boxes of bread accumulated on the porch, vegetable trim dried up on the ground.

Then on March 24, two weeks to the day, Josephine returned. She limped badly; the ankle of her left hind leg was swollen to twice its normal size. But Josephine was alive, and had come back to her paradise. Ed examined the ankle as best he could without a tranquilizer. From a distance of three or four feet, he could see no trap or snare, no cuts or breaks in the skin. His conjecture was that Josephine had bruised it, perhaps breaking through some sharp ice, or getting caught between two logs in the woods.

Now a semi-invalid, Josephine rated more care than ever, and naturally wiggled her way more deeply into every Dolney heart. No labor or sacrifice was too great for the lame pet. Josephine was fed and petted, even more devotedly than before.

By mid-May Josephine's ankle was greatly improved, and the limp was almost gone. She had imperceptibly become a member of the Dolney family, just about as dear as any human member.

However, with the coming of springtime, Josephine must again leave. Her feeding was discontinued.

The parting was quite like that of the previous May. Ann was busy planting and transplanting. Josephine came to her three times that day to have the black blanket of tormenting mosquitoes wiped from her nose and eyes. Nonetheless, she walked across the garden and into the sunset, gone for the summer.

Ed and Ann call their homestead Happy Acres. The name is appropriate. They created what they have with their own hands, cleared the land, jetted the well, and built the house, garage, greenhouse, etc. They are located eight miles west of Fairbanks. Ann's main love is her garden, where she raises and sells vegetables and flowers. When the ground is frozen solid outside and covered with snow, she beautifies the inside of her house with numerous potted plants.

The summer of '67 the garden grew especially well. Ann's green thumb produced 10-pound zucchini squash, 12-foot-tall sunflowers and several 30-pound cabbages. Most of the vegetables went to market, but all that the family could possibly use were stored in a cool corner of the basement.

Then Jack Frost came and did his color dance on the foliage. The deep freeze commenced in September. October winds tore off the leaves and piled up the snow. Spruce trees held out their arms to be filled with white stuff, and every twig clothed itself in sparkling crystal. The long, fierce, winter for which Alaska is famous had begun.

October passed, and the Dolneys became anxious for Josephine's return. They wondered how she had fared with the injured ankle. Had she been able to evade the wolves? Was she still alive? Would she remember?

On November 4th, Ann stood over the sink, looking out the kitchen window. Josephine erupted over the road, and rushed down the driveway, stopping only when her breath was on the window. Ann nearly burst with excitement, joy, and pride. She grabbed several packs of hamburger buns, and rushed out to feed her pet.

Josephine had not forgotten. For the third year, Jo had come home to the Dolneys. Josephine now stood seven feet tall and weighed in at about eight hundred pounds, but she was still as gentle as ever. Her lips often touched the hands that fed her, but no one had yet felt the bite of her teeth.

Friends and neighbors gathered for a New Year's Eve party at the Dolneys. At 11:59, one minute before midnight, Josephine appeared at the window. New Year's toasts were forgotten. There was a mad rush for cameras and flash bulbs. Only after Josephine was properly fed, and abundantly photographed, was the New Year ushered in.

Some mornings Josephine would be bedded down outside the big picture window. She often stood at Ann's bedroom window at 6:30 AM to watch Ann dress. Then she'd move over to the dining room window, and watch the family eat breakfast. The children delighted in feeding Jo before the school bus came. Slice by slice she would eat a loaf of bread from each hand.

Josephine was evidently more enamored with her human friends, than with her own kind. But she did get a boyfriend, a handsome fellow about three years old at the time, judging by his antlers. And like a dutiful daughter, she brought him home for the adopted parents to look over. But he was very wary of humans, not having been conditioned to their kindness as Jo was. Afraid, he stood far off, and watched Josephine eat loaf after loaf of bread. Finally, his resistance yielded and he started to join Jo, but then an automobile raced by and scared him away.

Josephine herself became heavy with calf. We could see it kick her sides occasionally. Soon she would, in the manner of wise moose mothers, seek out a shallow swamp where she could best protect herself and her calf.

There isn't a fence post or a foot of wire on the Dolney homestead. Josephine was free to come and go as she pleased. Indeed she did return for the following 13 winters!

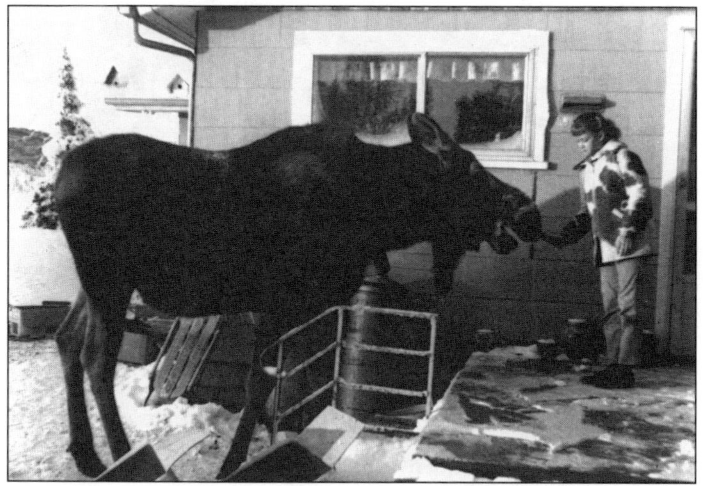

Vitalizing Your Alaska Experience

Attention Visitors: Don't Leave Alaska Without

An Adventure

The real Alaska lies beyond the major cities, off the beaten path. Make the most of your visit by experiencing thrills and chills that will make your heart sing and supply you with enough tall tales to last a lifetime.

There are things to see in Alaska that you can't see anywhere else. Come savor Alaska's authentic flavor and participate in an exciting adventure, a rare and exhilarating journey where the natural beauty and wonders are unparalleled.

Take home the beauty and grandeur of this land in snapshots and memories written indelibly on the walls of your heart. You will be glad you did.

Living an Alaskan Adventure

1. To really get in touch with the Alaskan wilderness and terrain, nothing beats a road trip through the state. One of the best is the **Dalton Highway**– a 414-mile gravel road that heads north from Livengood and ends at Prudhoe Bay. On this fantastic journey of a lifetime, you'll see the towering, rugged peaks of the Brooks Range, and pass Wiseman (an 1890's gold rush town), and through some of the most magnificent arctic tundra Alaska has to offer. The claim is that you will see more wildlife along the Dalton than in the famous Denali National Park! You'll view one of the most remarkable engineering feats of modern time: the 800-mile Trans-Alaska Pipeline. Learning how it was built to withstand the wide variation in Alaska temperatures, while causing minimal disruption to environment and wildlife, one begins to understand and appreciate the tremendous effort this achievement required.
2. Enjoy a trip to **Denali National Park** with its cold, flowing, picturesque rivers, rolling tundra and abundant wildlife. Denali is a scenic wonderland unmatched by anything on earth! View as many as possible of the 37 species of wildlife in their natural habitat on a rewarding, and often breathtaking, bus ride through the hidden areas inside the park. At the center of the six-million-acre park is the wondrous 20,320-foot Mount McKinley, the tallest peak in North America. One of Alaska's chief tourist attractions, it dominates the interior and is one of the most impressive features of the Alaska landscape. Over fifty percent of Mount McKinley is covered with permanent

snowfields, and glaciers surround its base. On a clear day, viewing the silent majesty of this snow-covered giant is an awesome sight.

3. Experience a **spring breakup** on the Yukon River. See and hear the creaking, shifting, crashing, and grinding of tons of ice breaking up and flowing out to sea. These powerful forces of nature immediately gain the respect of all present, and will live powerfully in your memory as one of the most awe-inspiring events to have witnessed.
4. Take a white water adventure on a raft or kayak down one of our many untamed rivers. It's wet, wild and exhilarating! Stand at the edge of a wilderness valley, or visit an Indian or Eskimo village.
5. Watch a traditional **fish wheel** in operation as it utilizes the forces of nature to pluck salmon out of the river and effortlessly deposit them in a storage box, and then onto the cleaning table and drying racks. It's Eskimo candy in the making!
6. Fairbanks hosts the **World Eskimo Indian Olympics**, a four-day series of traditional Alaska native athletic competitions and dances. The games take place in mid-July, in the Big Dipper Arena. Events such as the ear pull are rooted in practicality. In this event, two competitors are joined together by a piece of string looped around their ears, and seated face-to-face. The competition begins as the athletes pull away from each other, trying to keep the string around their ears, while bearing the pain that this action produces. If you win, your toughness and tolerance for pain amaze the fans. If you lose, you may lose more than just the game. Ears have actually been pulled off in this event! These games not only provide

entertainment, they also give men and women the strength, discipline and endurance they need to survive in a harsh and unforgiving climate. Visitors will see unparalleled feats of endurance and agility. It is a rare chance to experience a culture alongside those who live within it.

7. Take in the **Golden Days celebrations** in Fairbanks, where the past comes back to life each mid-July. See the can-can dancers and the parade. Try your luck and bet on the Rubber Duckie Race, as the ducks float down the Chena River. Eat your fill of sourdough pancakes at the pancake feed and share in the revival of the gold rush days.
8. **Fishing** is hot at the Kenai River, which is world famous for its salmon runs. Catching, fighting and landing a king salmon is a thrill you won't soon forget. The world record is 97 pounds, 4 ounces.
9. Warm up in one of the Interior's **natural hot springs**. Not only do the hot springs offer a unique natural phenomena, many of the resorts offer rental cabins in these beautiful settings for hiking, camping, biking, hunting, fishing and winter activities.
10. Visit Katmai National Park, now famous for being a **bear watchers'** haven. At the peak of July's sockeye salmon run, as many as 40 bears inhabit the Brooks River drainage, and offer the visitor one of the best bear bonanzas!
11. Travel the miles of **hiking and biking** trails through the state to see and explore. Some of the best experiences happen spontaneously on this exciting frontier as you enjoy nature in its ultimate glory.

12. Pick up a **gold pan** and head to the creeks. Folks are still finding gold nuggets and flakes. Panning your own gold nuggets will be the highlight of any day in Alaska, and sometimes the rewards can pay for your entire trip!
13. Watch the creeks and rivers turn color with struggling **salmon** in their dogged attempt to return to their spawning grounds.
14. Wander out into a **blueberry** patch and enjoy some of the biggest and best-tasting blueberries the world has to offer. Even the bears love them!
15. Valdez, just outside the Kenai National Wildlife Refuge, is known for some of the best **fishing** in the state; it is a mecca for saltwater anglers. In more recent years, Valdez has also developed as a center for extreme sports, and is currently home of the World Extreme Skiing Championships. Valdez additionally offers mountain biking, ice climbing, kayaking and whitewater rafting for the more daring of its visitors.
16. The **glaciers** and awesome **icebergs** off coastal waters present one of the most memorable and wondrous spectacles available to the Alaskan visitor. Two of Alaska's more than 5000 glaciers, the Bering and the Malaspina are bigger than the state of Delaware. The two most visited glacier attractions in Alaska are the Portage and Mendenhall. Icebergs are formed when ice breaks off a glacier into a body of water (it's called calving). The sheer size, force, and of course, the thunderous crashing of glaciers falling into the sea, is a sight and sound not to be missed!
17. Join in **taking the plunge** in Nome. Much of the city of Nome turned out for the city's Memorial Day 1996 Polar

Bear Swim. More than 140 adventurous souls took a holiday dip in the Bering Sea in 32-degree water. The swimmers had to contend with ice and small icebergs. You will remember this adventure for a long time.

18. Observe the **geese** gathering their young in the fall of the year. Watch as they honk, circle, and climb up from their summer home, to assemble in a V formation pointed south, and go to where they can fly in warmer skies. Geese are very intelligent birds.
19. Just outside of Anchorage is Mt. Alyeska, the state's best ski resort. For the **skiing and snow-boarding** enthusiast, Alyeska is an absolute must!
20. For serious winter travelers, **mushing a team of dogs** (the former traditional mode of transportation in Alaska) affords a true appreciation of the Alaskan way of life. It offers a oneness with nature and a better understanding of Alaska in all its white, wintertime glory. If you would rather watch, we have the 1,000-mile Iditarod Sled Dog Race from Wasilla to Nome. The Yukon Quest, billed as the "Challenge of the North," is a 1,000-mile run between Fairbanks and Whitehorse in Canada. The "Granddaddy of Sprint Races," the Open North American Championship Sled Dog Race takes place in March over three days, with 20-mile and 30-mile heats that begin and end in Fairbanks.
21. Have a **Snowmobile Adventure:** A snowmobile (or snowmachine) is a motorized vehicle designed to carry people on top of the snow, over the once-inaccessible snowbound countryside. To people in rural areas, a snowmobile is a vehicle that provides transportation for hunting, hauling firewood and water, plus fun and recreation every snow day.

22. Envision yourself racing over the snow, the course flooded with light from the Aurora Borealis. Many city residents utilize the **snowmobile** for weekend excursions and trail riding with family and friends; but for farmers, loggers, power line crews, conservation officers, police, trappers, and others, the snowmobile is an everyday work vehicle.
23. See the northland phenomenon-the midnight ballet of the **Northern Lights** in rippling, shimmering displays as the shapes and colors dance in the northern skies.
24. See the world-famous ice sculptures at the annual International **Ice Sculptures** Competition and Exhibition. These Ice Art Championships always start the first Wednesday of March in Fairbanks. Some of the mammoth sculptures reach over 20 feet in height and are a marvel of modern sculpting, with amazing detail and intricacies. See them at night when colorful lights sparkle through the sculptures.

More Captivating Adventures

Tinkerbell Joins Us for Lunch

By Christa Crisman

My husband Paul, daughter Michelle, and I enjoy having guests share meals with us. What makes this story different is that our favorite guest, Tinkerbell, is a young moose. Maybe the first moose ever to join a family for meals, with her own place setting at the table. And no, her table manners were not good. Actually, she didn't have any. Although we offered repeatedly, she never sat down to eat at the table; she preferred to just poke her head through the open window. She took big bites of everything that she could reach, gobbling her food, knocking things over, and slobbering everywhere. She never talked, just snorted and made moose noises, but she was good company. I loved to gaze into her large, smiling, brown eyes from a few feet away, and watch her eat everything she could reach. This was such a great honor to me; the thrill and bubbly feeling captivated my emotions. Not only to be accepted by this wild moose, but to have the added joy of sharing a meal with a big animal right at our kitchen table. During every visit Tinkerbell was the sole center of attention until she had enough to eat, or we ran out of food. Then she would graciously leave and step back into the wilderness.

The record snowfall in 1970, totaling 168 inches, created hardships for the moose. Their usual forage was inaccessible, covered by the deep snow. Thus, many animals were starving and dying.

What first attracted this moose was Michelle's horse, Star, as well as the hay. Star was kept in a corral, and Paul and Michelle would carry armfuls of hay to keep Star well fed. They often dropped hay along the path to the corral. This moose would come along and clean up all she could get.

Now when I first noticed this starving young moose from my kitchen window, and saw how thin it was, my heart just melted. One day I opened the window, not knowing quite what to expect but wanting to help, and I held out a head of lettuce. Hunger-driven and void of fear, the yearling moose eagerly came and ate ravenously, as though this was her first meal in weeks.

In the days that followed our mutual trust and friendship grew, and I named the moose Tinkerbell. Tinkerbell kept returning for her daily window feeding, most days starting at 6:00 AM and ending at 12:00 PM. To keep up, our family began visiting the grocery stores to pick up any scrap produce they had to feed this moose.

Soon, our story of Tinkerbell was in the newspaper and on the radio. People from all over the lower 48 states were sending letters of good wishes and money to help feed this hungry animal. Tinkerbell was eating up to 40 pounds of food a day when she could get it. She loved bread, lettuce, bananas, apples, and pretty much anything we put in front of her! I remember one day this hungry moose ate up the last six loaves of bread in the house. My poor husband Paul had to go without bread in his lunch that day.

Now, the Fish & Game folks did not approve of us feeding Tinkerbell. They said she would die anyway, many already had; but by now Tinkerbell was one of our family. She became friendly with Star and began sleeping alongside the corral.

When the thermostat dropped to 50° below zero I had to make an effort to keep her food from freezing solid. The only way I could do that was to open my kitchen window and let her stick her head in to eat off the kitchen table. These open-window lunch affairs caused the heat bill to go up by over $50 that month. Tinkerbell continued coming for four months until spring, when heat from the sun's rays melted the snow and she could forage for herself.

She returned the following winter but had grown so big that she couldn't fit her head in the kitchen window anymore. As I look back over my years in Alaska, one of my fondest memories is that I was accepted by Tinkerbell and the entertaining meals that we shared.

A One Hundred-Foot-High Chunk of Ice

By Ken Elbert

As the moving mountain of water got closer, I was sure our boat would be swamped and I thought I was going to die.

I was a teenager seeking work and adventure the summer of 1978. I finagled a job on my neighbor Fred's 32-foot commercial fishing boat in the Gulf of Alaska.

It didn't take me long to discover that I didn't like the job at all. Seasick most of the time, always wet and cold, slipping and falling on the wet deck, handling slimy fish, getting yelled at for not moving fast enough, working 12-to-16 hours a day-it was just not my idea of a fun work experience. I was the one in our four-man crew who most welcomed the news from Fish and Game over the ship's radio, the temporary emergency closure of fishing.

Since we couldn't fish, we decided to go looking for excitement, anything to improve our low morale. Fred headed for the huge Columbia Glacier. This glacier towered over a hundred feet above us and the ocean. We watched from 70 feet away as a few small ice chunks fell off the glacier and made big splashes. This was exciting, but it seemed like a long time between splashes, and we were getting impatient for more action. Fred decided to hurry things up a bit by shooting at the glacier with a rifle. We were hoping the noise would cause more chunks of ice to fall and make a big splash. Little did we imagine how successful we would be. Two shots later, a 50-foot-wide, 100-foot-high chunk of ice slowly started to break away. It was spectacular to watch as it slid into the water in slow motion. But it made an enormous splash. We saw a tremendous wave forming, and I began to worry as it headed straight toward us. Fred watched the wall of seawater rise up in front of us, and in desperation he turned the boat so that it faced the oncoming tidal wave. I began to pray. As the moving mountain of water got closer, it looked to be 40-to-50 feet high, and I was sure that the boat would be swamped. Then it was upon us. The boat headed straight up the mountain size wave, then plunged straight down the other side. All I could see was water. My stomach was in my throat. I thought we were going under and we would drown. Instead, the boat rode up the next wave and down the other side, just like a giant roller coaster. Each new wave grew gradually weaker. We hung on and rode them out. It seemed like ten minutes went by before Fred calmed down enough to turn the boat. We left Glacier Bay but kept a wary eye over our shoulder, lest another wave overtake us. We had enough adventure for one day.

I learned two lessons that summer. "I didn't want to be a commercial fisherman and don't mess with a glacier."

I Saw a Moose Climbing Up a Tree

By Bob Morse

Everyone but the moose knows, moose can't climb.

One bitter, cold winter morning a few years ago, I was nursing my cantankerous old pickup down our rural road. Getting to work on time was my intent. Through the ice fog, my bleary eyes were searching for the contours of the road, now buried under a three-inch blanket of new snow.

Suddenly off to the left, movement of something dark against the white landscape captured my attention. There was this moose in a birch tree, not 50 feet off the road. I could hardly believe my eyes. I stomped on the brakes and skidded to a stop. Everyone knows moose can't climb trees! But right in front of me was this gangling monster with her long front legs stretching up over the higher branches of a birch tree. She was up on tiptoes with just her hind hoofs touching the ground. As she reached higher and higher for the tender shoot at the ends of the higher branches, her back legs left the ground, and the young birch tree was supporting her entire weight. She was suspended there between heaven and earth, her hind legs kicking wildly. I would have traded my truck for a camera that day just to record what I was seeing.

I couldn't afford to be late to work, but I watched as long as I could before leaving the moose eating and kicking, up in that tree. The next eight hours dragged by at work, as I looked forward to re-checking the moose scene. When I returned that night, the moose wasn't anywhere around.

Robert Service, in his narration, "The Cremation of Sam McGee" tells about the strange things done in the midnight sun and the northern lights having seen queer sights. But the sun nor the northern lights were out to see what I saw: that moose climbing a tree.

We Could Have Frozen to Death

By Diane Hallett

Before Our Honeymoon

Monday night, December 27, 1985 will forever be emblazoned on my mind. In tears of surrender to God's will, I prayed for a lifemate of His choosing. The next day at noon, Mark walked into my life–and that evening at a company Christmas party, we discussed marriage!

Seventy-five days later, on the afternoon of March 2nd at the Pump House Restaurant near Fairbanks, God united our hearts as one. Pastor Don Brandon, from his wheelchair, married us in a room filled with gold mining equipment and frontier décor. A full evening of celebrating with family and friends followed. Then the two of us headed for Chena Hot Springs Resort, 60 miles from town.

It was a coal-black night and the temperature dropped to 40° below zero, but we felt warm in each other's company. For 40 minutes we blithely tooled along the frosty, tree-lined road that had only an occasional dwelling. Suddenly, we were startled by a loud clunking noise from under the hood, and the engine died. We were enveloped in darkness, dressed in our wedding finery, and definitely not prepared to contend with the elements! We hadn't seen another car or building for some time. No one else would be traveling to the Hot Springs at this late hour. Stories I'd heard since childhood of people freezing to death in similar situations flooded my mind. With hearts full of faith we prayed to Jesus for help!

Before our car rolled to a complete stop we saw headlights in the distance. Jumping out of our car as this lone car drew closer, we waved like our life depended on it-which it did.

Upon slowing down, stopping, and hearing our dilemma, this kind couple offered to drive us back to Angel Creek Lodge, from where they had just come. Once inside we told our story to the bartender, several crusty-looking miners, and a middle-aged couple wearing fox fur hats. A miner wearing red suspenders called out "Free drinks for the house!" and our celebration continued.

As the night wore on, the miners all departed and the big-hearted couple with the fur hats offered to take us the additional ten miles to the Hot Springs. Finally in our rented cabin, we snuggled down in warmth and safety for the remainder of our honeymoon night. Thanks to God and some generous Alaskans we were not fighting for our lives in a broken-down car on a deserted road during a forty-below Alaskan night.

Sam Turned White as A Sheet

By Pete Atkins

I took my friend and co-worker Sam, a black man with me to Chitina, to dip for the wily salmon in the Copper River. Filled with suspended silt, the swift currents of the glacier-fed Copper River make it one of Alaska's most dangerous rivers. Every year thousands of dippers like myself wade into the current to sift the murky waters with a dip net, hoping to catch salmon. Sam and I crawled down the steep cliffs and over the slippery rocks in Wood Canyon to reach our favorite spot. The wind was blowing sand in our faces as we searched for a back-eddy, which are usually caused by the big rocks jutting out in the silt-laden river. We found our spot and soon caught several salmon. Sam kept on dipping, and I climbed back up to the truck to clean the fish we had caught, before we had more than I could carry up the bank.

I had just opened the fourth salmon when Sam commenced screaming for help. I rushed down the bank to see what the problem was and to help him. Sam had a big King salmon in his net that was trying to pull him in the river. They were both fighting for their very lives. With one hand, Sam had a vise-like hold on a tree limb and was hanging on for dear life. The other hand was holding the dip net. Another dip-netter also rushed over and we both grabbed hold of Sam, pulling him to safety and helped him get the King landed. You've all heard stories of someone being so scared they turned white as a sheet. Well, there was my friend Sam, white as a sheet.

Bears are a Threat in the Blueberry Patch

By Nadine Berka

I shot over the bear, to scare her, but my gun didn't work.

On his way out the door my husband Lew flashed me his cutest "Please dear" smile when he asked me, "Hon, make me a blueberry pie for supper." So I called two lady friends, and we went out blueberry picking. I always wear my .357 handgun when out picking because bears are a fact of life and a threat to anyone in the blueberry patch. We had seen a mother bear and two cubs earlier in the day, but far off. There were other folks picking berries in the patch that I had selected just off the road near the Fort Knox Gold Mine. I had told all the people not to worry because I had a gun and I knew how to use it. We were all busy picking berries, when I happened to look up. Mother bear was reared up on her hind legs, one 100 feet away. Exerting a great effort to be calm, I squealed "B E A R." After regaining my composure and trying to be as brave as I thought I sounded, I told everyone to slowly go back to their cars, and I would stay there and watch to make sure that the bear didn't follow anyone. I stood ready to fire a shot if she moved closer to scare her away, but not to kill her. Mother bear started toward me, so I pointed the gun over her head and fired. Nothing happened! I pulled the trigger again and again, still nothing–all misfiring! I felt so foolish, me the big protector. I knew this was a bad situation and that it was time for me to leave, too. I grabbed my half-full blueberry bucket and headed for the car. Luckily, the bear dropped down on all four paws and returned to eating. She was more interested in filling up on tasty blueberries, and she didn't follow me.

When I got home I checked out my .357 and found it rusted up. I had carried it through too many wet excursions without cleaning and oiling it. A glance at the clock told me that it was time to make a blueberry pie, if I wanted to keep Lew smiling at me. That night after a supper of warmed-up moose stew, I served Lew his favorite dessert-blueberry pie. The look of pleasure on his face spread like the stain from the blueberries around his mouth and I felt pleased. But Lew's happy look changed to concern and worry, when I told him about my day berry picking, the bear, and my gun being rusted. My caring husband reminded me that not taking care of your equipment can cost you your life. He added, "I don't want to lose the girl I love, and the best blueberry pie maker in Alaska, to a bear."

This Bear Was So Close

By Ron Webb

I Could See His Nostrils Flare

Humans and bears are both attracted to rivers during the salmon run, causing some close encounters. In 1990 I was fishing in a stream in south central Alaska. It was in July, about 2:00 AM, and I was alone. I was wearing hip waders and I was out about 20 feet from the bank when a grizzly bear came trotting toward me. He stopped on the bank at my tackle box. He was so close I could see his nostrils flare when he sniffed the salmon roe I was using for bait. I backed away into the stream just a little too far, causing my waders to fill with water. The bear stood on his hind legs, and it sure looked to me like he thought I was a ham sandwich! He said "WOOF"! I spoke to him in low tones and did my very best to make friends. After what seemed like a very long time, he left. Must have figured I would taste like I *smelled.*

Statehood Bill Passed and Alaska was Celebrating

By Mrs. Jo Papp

Coming to Alaska had been my dream since the colored maps in my fifth grade geography book coaxed my thoughts away from a Pennsylvania home to the far north, and a place that I have now called home for the last 40 years–Fairbanks.

Alaska became the 49th state two days after my arrival in 1958 at the University of

Alaska, on the outskirts of Fairbanks. Some of us students were sitting together getting acquainted. Early in the afternoon of June 30 someone came running down the hall in Wickersham dorm shouting, "Congress just passed the Statehood Bill! Find a ride; everyone is going into Fairbanks!"

My roommate Jan and I lost no time joining the crowds who were exiting the building. We piled into one of the many student cars-turned-into-taxi-service, and followed the traffic that headed toward town. Fairbanks was filled with people and vehicles. There was no way to drive across the Chena River; the bridge into town was plugged with non-moving cars. Our driver found a place to park near Samson's Hardware Store, on the north side of the river. We got out and hurried to the walking path on the Iron Bridge. There, we joined others watching a person wading into the river upstream. He was pouring dye into the crystal-clear water of the Chena. His plan was to transform the river into a golden color–for Fairbanks was the Golden Heart City.

The dye did change the color of the water as it spread and drifted downstream. But instead of turning the river golden, it turned it an inappropriate putrid green. The crowd lining the bridge and banks of the river began to laugh and shout and cheer.

An impromptu parade formed, made up of cars and trucks jammed full of cheering bodies. Horns honked and vehicles collected more celebrants. The parade circled First and Second Avenues between Cushman and Lacey Streets. Those that lined the streets called greetings to people they recognized. One name that got everyone's attention was that of Governor Mike Stepovich, who rode in a big truck, and looked as happy as those calling out to him.

Every business seemed to have its doors wide open. People flowed in and out, talking, cheering, and enjoying the moment. Some doorways led into bars where the flow of people slowed down, and beer bottles clanked numerous toasts to the occasion.

On Cushman Street, a long line formed. Residents were writing their thank you messages to Congress for the momentous vote that had been taken a few hours earlier, a vote that forever changed Alaska from a territory into the 49th state!

We headed back to the university, happy and exhausted. It had been exciting and wonderful fun to be part of the spontaneous celebration. No one could have planned a better beginning to my life in Alaska.

**To meet Jo and her husband John, you can stop by the Tanana Valley Farmers' Market at the fairgrounds in Fairbanks on Wednesdays, 11 AM to 4 PM, and Saturdays 9 AM to 4 PM, and buy some of their fresh Alaskan vegetables.*

Alaska Flag Song

Eight stars of gold on a field of blue
Alaska's flag, may it mean to you
The blue of the sea, the evening sky,
The mountain lakes and the flowers nearby;
The gold of the early sourdough's dreams,
The precious gold of the hills and streams,
The brilliant stars in the northern sky,
The Bear, the Dipper, and shinning high,
The great north star with its steady light,
Over land and sea a beacon bright,
Alaska's flag - to Alaskans dear,
The simple flag of a last frontier.

Marie Drake

Lenny's Dream Was to Shoot a Moose

By Paul Elbert

The problem: Lenny was paralyzed from the waist down.

September 10th the potatoes were harvested and stored in the bulging bins of my root cellar. I was looking forward to moose hunting in my favorite area, the place I call the Trophy Pasture. I had a close friend named Lenny, who before an accident was also an avid hunter. But now he was bound to a wheelchair, paralyzed from the waist down. During the previous winter Lenny and I had often talked about hunting, and his biggest dream was to shoot a moose. I wanted to help Lenny achieve his dream.

I figured out a way to take him moose hunting along with my son and two soldier friends. We all had moose tags. I drove Lenny and one soldier in; we crossed the Savage River in my old pickup truck. My son and the other soldier had rented horses for hunting the hills, and were riding the horses in. We set up camp beside a wide spot in the trail about 50 feet in from a ledge that overlooked the *Trophy Pasture.*

Early next morning, I woke everyone at first light. We got

Lenny up and in his wheelchair, and one soldier rolled him to a prime spot overlooking this meadow. The other soldier, my son and I had rounded up the horses and were putting the saddles on, getting ready for our big hunt. Just then we heard a shot, and the soldier came running back shouting, "Lenny shot a moose." Then we heard another shot, and we all ran to see what that was all about. There was Lenny, sitting straight and proud in his wheelchair, just beaming. Lenny broke into a smile and the happiness just exploded from his face.

Lenny shouted out, "I shot two moose, the big one for you, Paul." He went on, "When I first got to the ledge, it was scarcely light enough to see; but I could make out a cow moose walking across the meadow, and then I noticed a young bull following her. I shot the bull, and the cow just kept walking away. Then another big bull came out of the brush, following after the cow, so I shot him too. He's yours, Paul."

We spent that day butchering and hanging the meat. The hunt was over.

Lenny died the following year, and I miss him, but I have always felt good about helping him achieve his one big dream.

An Unworldly, Tortured Screeching Split the Silence

By Michael Crews

Running the crab pots never gets boring–each day becomes a separate adventure. Nature displays new landscapes with each ever-changing mood of the sun–sunrise, brilliant sunshine, sunsets, northern lights, sundogs, rainbows, storms, mirages, and wildlife scenes.

I supplement my meager income during the long winter by commercial crabbing. I venture out on the frozen Bering Sea from Nome with my snowmobile, pulling a sled full of gear and crab pots. Finding a likely looking spot, I stop and begin cutting a hole through the nearly three feet of ice. I use a special homemade, hand-held, large chisel-type tool to chip away at the ice. I make my holes about five-feet-by-five-feet, and it would take me between two and three hours to complete each hole. I also make my own crab pots. The crab pots are limited in size and style only by the ambition (and condition) of the fisherman. I pull the rope attached to the crab pot hand-over-hand, from 50-to-80-foot depths. Working alone, and in the minus 20 degree cold, a crab-laden pot can quickly become exceedingly heavy to the unseasoned.

On warmer days, I would take my two-year-old son Nick out with me to pull the pots. His big, blue eyes, cherry-red cheeks, and blond curly hair seemed to fit right in with the glistening, white seascape. Already experienced in crab handling, he transported them–one crab at a time–by the hind leg from pot to sled.

Running the crab pots never gets boring. Each day becomes a separate adventure. Nature displays new landscapes with each ever-changing mood of the sun–sunrise, brilliant sunshine, sunsets, northern lights, sundogs, rainbows, storms, mirages, and wildlife scenes. The beauty and imagery constantly keeps one alert and in awe. In the distance, a dark spot grows into a seal basking itself on flat surface ice as you near. A pair of red foxes eye you warily from a pressure ridge as you pass, and ravens occasionally dive down to the ice for a spied morsel.

One painfully cold morning, I approached my set and shut off the snowmobile. I was greeted by the terrifying sound of cascading water. Suddenly, I realized that the water level had dropped under the ice, and I was standing atop a ceiling some feet above the water. The crashing cascade was the surf pounding against stalactites hanging down under the ice. The sound was amplified in the brittle air. Part of the ice shelf had broken off and was being floated along in the current. As the moving ice contacted the stationary surface, an unworldly, tortured, screeching split the silence. I hurriedly heaved my rope, pots, and dozen-or-so-claw-waving crabs up on the sled and departed.

Another time I attempted to follow a snowmobile trail out on the ice; however, visibility was greatly reduced by a driving sleet storm. Blowing right into our faces, the snow stung like BB shot. Straining to see, I topped a pressure ridge and stopped. I had lost the trail, so I got off to look around. Suddenly, the whole world under my feet began to buckle and heave sickeningly. One glance at the undulating seascape was enough to convince me to seek more secure surroundings. I made a flying leap for my snowmobile and a run for the beach.

I Don't Eat'em That Kind, He Got Shoes On

By Ann Dolney

Our family of four was living in Wiseman for the summer, and next door lived Louisa, a young Native girl. Now Louisa was a couple of years older than my two little girls, but they played together all the time. The mail plane would come in just once every two weeks, and this time friends had sent us some fresh pork chops, which were quite a treat for us. We usually just made do with what we had brought with us: canned food, etc. My older daughter Linda ran in and asked if Louisa could stay for dinner. I said sure. So, we were all sitting around the table enjoying our pork chops. Louisa was enjoying hers, cutting it off in front of her mouth Eskimo style, when she looked up and said "Ann, what kind this one?" meaning the meat. She said, "No moose, no caribou, no sheep, no bear, what kind?" She went through all the meats she knew, and it wasn't any of those. I told her pig, and she said, "What's pig?" I told her pork, and she said, "What's that?" So I found the children's picture book with Porky the Pig in it. Porky was all dressed up in this picture, and when I showed it to Louisa saying, "Here is a pig" her eyes got as big as saucers. She pushed her plate away and said, "I don't eat'em that kind; he got shoes on."

Out In Front of Our Igloo

By Sam Webb

We were in our swimsuits, sitting in lawn chairs, out in front of our igloo.

On a Boy Scout camping trip our troop went to Turnagain Pass in Anchorage. I was one of the senior scouts, and every March we went to build snow caves. This year we decided to build an igloo out of hard-packed snow that was just like ice.

We used a saw to cut the blocks of ice, and started stacking them up. Six of us worked for the next 14 hours to complete the igloo. It was fairly warm, about 20 degrees. We built ours close to the road, and for fun we put out pink flamingos that we had brought, as well as lawn chairs, and a beach umbrella. We put on our swimsuits and were in the lawn chairs sipping lemonade just like we would on a sandy beach.

The first people that came by were tourists, and they couldn't believe what they saw. They stopped and came over to talk to us. They asked if we were Eskimos, and if this was the way we lived all winter, etc. We really got a kick out of their reaction to what appeared to be our lifestyle in the cold north.

-Encouragement for dogs pulling a dog sled-

Strive to be the lead dog, else the scenery never changes.

Life In The Village of Kalskag

By Harold Thompson

It's not unusual in Lower Kalskag to have grandma and grandpa, sons and daughters, husbands, wives and children, all living in the same house.

My father-in-law is one of the elders. His Bible is written in the Russian language, or Slovanic. He can speak English, Central Yup'ik, and Russian Slovanic. When he spoke, he spoke in Yup'ik and Russian Slovanic. Nobody could understand the Russian Slavic, except people his age (he's almost 80). Those 40 years old or older could under-stand the Yup'ik. The kids couldn't understand any of it. But they sat there attentively and quietly. They were patient, and they watched, because they have a lot of respect for the elders. The elders run the village and make the decisions. You are not an elder when you're 40 or 50. You have to be 70 or 80 to be considered somebody that has wisdom and respect, enough so that your wishes are considered to be the most important.

I don't think money is very important in Kalskag. There

are very few jobs in the village. You have schoolteachers, but none of them are ever born in Kalskag, because no one who's been born there has graduated from college.

There are jobs for a few people, but not very many. Firefighting during the fire season is one of the biggest sources of income in the village. People get money from their Permanent Fund dividend, and from whatever aid they may qualify for from our state and federal governments, because they live below the poverty level. But money is not as important in the village as it is in the city. There is not much to buy, because there are no stores that sell the commodities that are available in the cities. You and I use money to buy food. They use a bullet, a snare, a trap, or a net to get food.

They do need money for their snowmobiles and fuel. Every family has a snowmobile, costing three or four thousand dollars. They might have pooled their resources from their dividend checks. Then the biggest sons and the father can run a trapline and hunt.

They all used to have little log homes that they built themselves. Lower Kalskag actually was taken away by the Kuskokwim River and had to be rebuilt. In the seventies, the state and federal governments, through different agencies, provided money and modern homes with running water.

The old log houses were small, and the people had big families. It's not unusual in Lower Kalskag to have grandma and grandpa, sons and daughters, husbands, wives and children, all living in the same house. The young kids will sleep in bed with their parents or right there on the floor, and everybody's together. That's normal. If your son is 40 and he has two or three kids, for him to live with his mother and father, his wife, and even some of his brothers and sisters all in the same house is perfectly normal. The family unit stays together and it works.

My father-in-law's house has a wood stove. It's right in the middle of the living room. But he wasn't using it. He's burning oil, just like everybody else. He has a cache outside his house: a little, miniature log cabin that's built three or four feet off the ground with nice big, thick logs, and a big door, with a big padlock. And inside that cache is also a three-foot deep reserve of dry fish.

My father-in-law raised 11 children. He goes out to his fish camp every year. He has eight daughters and three sons, and some combination of those children and his wife go to fish camp. They work while the fish are running in June and July. The family catching their fish with hand-held gill net, bringing them to shore in his boat. He built three boats, all made of wood. They put the net out, and they let it drift for a few minutes along where the current is coming in. Then they pull it in by hand. They throw all the salmon into the boat, and when they have a load of 20 or 30, they take 'em ashore and put 'em in another little net along shore. Then the women take an ulu, an Eskimo knife, and cut the fish. They take the bone out of it, and the head and the tail, and cut it and spread the meat open. Then they put notches in the meat, and hang it on wooden poles in the sun to dry. Some of it they dry completely in the sun, and that's how it is processed. Others they put in the smokehouse. They take little willow trees that are dry, and they burn the willow and smoke the fish. They make hundreds of pounds of preserved fish. It's a gourmet food to us, but to them it's the most normal thing in the world. They'll eat dried salmon all year.

Even though the newer houses have showers and bathtubs, people still prefer to clean themselves in the traditional way, which is in their steambath. Every house has a steam bath, which is what we would call a sauna. Now, my mother and father-in-law's house has a bathtub and shower, but they don't use it. They go out to their steambath every evening. The women only go with the women, and the men only go with the men. They heat it up and they get a good sweat going. They have buckets of water in there, and soap, and wash rags, and towels. And that's how they bathe. They stick a washcloth in a cold bucket of water that they draw out of the river, or out of their faucet, and they wash themselves with nice cold water because it's probably 100 degrees in the sauna/steambath. And they rinse themselves off with cold water. It's very refreshing. They get real hot in there, and they step outside into the cold air. They go back and forth. It's more than just getting clean. It's a way that they relax; it's the way that they socialize. Men socialize with the men, and the women relax with the women. Yup'iks have been doing that for hundreds and hundreds of years.

They are people that have a well-established culture and tradition. Yup'iks have been introduced to our Western culture, and they incorporated aspects of it into their own lifestyle that would be economically and socially convenient, and feasible for them. But they still cling to the parts of their lifestyle that they prefer.

Alaska Natives will always hunt and fish. They used to do it with mukluks, snowshoes, snares, and spears. When bullets, guns and snowmobiles came along, they would use the best technology available to do the same thing they've always done. They're going to get a moose to eat. They're all natural biologists and weathermen. They look at the clouds, and they know what kind of weather is going to come.

The kids go to school and learn reading, writing, and arithmetic, and the name of the president, etc., but it really doesn't affect them. The important thing is to respect your elders, and learn how to hunt and fish and gather.

In the evening, in Lower Kalskag, the kids are all out on their snowmobiles, on their four-wheelers, maybe a 15-year-old or a 13-year-old on the four-wheeler, and then behind it there's a sled. And there will be four-five-and six-year-olds on the sled; the big kids pull the little kids. They play, and they're not worried about the time either. Those kids are sometimes out there at 3:00 or 4:00 in the morning, at least during Slavic. Of course, they didn't have school that week. The school recognizes that that's their big holiday, so they're up all week, and they don't care about time. You don't have to worry about your kid getting run over by a car, or getting kidnapped or stolen, or anything. It's safe there. It's a warm little place to live; a simple lifestyle, and you don't want to go to college because you don't need to. You go to school because you want to learn, but you just kind of stay in Kalskag all your life. People don't move out because they don't want or need to. They're a happy lot; they hunt and fish and stay together in a family.

Celebrating Slavic in Kalskag

By Harold Thompson

The temperature was 45° below zero the morning we left Fairbanks.

The day we started the trip to Kalskag, the early morning hours were spent digging my old car out of the snow bank I had slid into two weeks earlier. All that time it just sat, froze-up, soaking up cold.

The next hour was spent applying heat, electric and open flame from a propane burner, before the engine would turn over. With added help from a jumper battery, it eventually started.

My four-wheel-drive car's front CV joint was broken, so the front wheels wouldn't drive. But I was able to put it in four-wheel drive and the back wheels turned. This is how I drove my wife and baby from Fairbanks to Anchorage because it was cheaper than flying, and I was kind of broke. My family and I flew from Anchorage to Aniak, which is a large village on the Kuskokwim River. At Aniak, we got in a tiny two-seater plane and took a 15-minute flight down the Kuskokwim River to Kalskag.

Christmas begins on January 6 and ends on January 13 in Kalskag. Then they celebrate New Year's on January 14. The reason that their New Year's and Christmas fall on different dates than ours is because their church (Russian Orthodox) uses a different calendar. They go by the Julian calendar; they never adopted the Gregorian calendar, under which we function.

When we arrived, Slavic had already begun. It starts at the church. There are big stars that are about three feet wide, all decorated, made out of little pieces of wood and garland and beads. They spin on a little point. A young person, like an altar boy in the church, takes the star out of the church and everybody follows him to a house. At that house, the young boy stands in the house and spins the star, and he continually spins it the whole time that the townspeople are in this house.

The townspeople go to every house in the village. In fact, they go to most of them twice over the seven-day period. While this young man is there spinning the star, all the people in the whole village who are awake go into this house until it's jam-packed and they're sticking out the doors. They sing songs in Russian, Yup'ik, or English, but mostly in Yup'ik. The songs are Russian Orthodox Christmas carols translated into Yup'ik. Then, when they're done singing after about 20 or 30 minutes, whoever owns the house asks somebody to say a few words. It's usually one of the elders or oldest persons in the family. They stand there and speak in the Yup'ik language to everybody there, knowing that almost everyone under the age of 30 cannot understand them.

But the older people can understand it, and the speech is given, and it's usually something about the Bible, or goodness, or honesty. It's a lesson being taught to the kids by the elders.

Then, when that talk is done, they start the feast. They put a big rug on the floor, and they invite all the people who aren't from the village, as well as the elders to kneel down. They eat a feast of all kinds of native food, berries, pies, cakes, coffee, tea, and juices. There is no alcohol in the village at all. Their tradition is that the first group of people that come to the floor to eat wait until every single person is done eating, and then that whole group of people gets up, and the second group of people comes to eat. They just eat, and eat until everyone is full and I got stuffed.

At the feast, I had porcupine meat and, of course, every kind of fish: salmon, trout, burbot and pike. We ate a lot of pike. There was seal meat from downriver and seal oil; there was bear meat; and, of course, moose and caribou meat. I even ate beaver tail and beaver feet. There were many soups: they had goose soup, duck soup, and moose soup. There was no beef, there was no chicken, no Spam, no sardines, no ham, nothing that we Westerners normally eat. It was all subsistence foods that the people had hunted, gathered, and saved for Slavic.

There were lots of sweets, and everything was homemade. They had pies that were made of bread; they also had meat pies, and Russian pies. It was wonderful food. There weren't many vegetables, but plenty of meat, pastries, and cakes.

Then they pass out gifts or candy. All the kids, adults, and elders have a sack with them. They fill the sacks up with these candies, or Ramen Noodle soups, work gloves, little pairs of scissors, or nail files. I got two pairs of work gloves, a little pair of scissors, and a little thermometer. Somebody gave out socks once–70-to-80 pairs of socks. After the gifts, the elders decide that it's time to go. The people at the next house down the street are ready. So the young boy takes the star, which was hung from the ceiling when the feast began, walks out of the house, and everyone follows him to the next house. He begins to spin the star, the singing starts, and they do it all over again. They do this from about 10:00 in the morning, all through the day until the wee hours of the morning, and then they finally take the star back to the church. People go to their homes, get a few hours of rest, then get right up and say, "Where is that star going today?" They go to the church, wait for the boy to come and get the star, and then follow him to the first house that day, which is the next house after where they left off. They go through every single person's house in Lower Kalskag and they sing, hear a talk from the elders, eat like crazy, and receive a gift. Then they go on to the next house. Because I can't understand Yup'ik, I couldn't comprehend their songs, or what the elder was saying.

It was terrific, but after the first three or four days, I decided that I'd rather sleep than continually do this. The stamina of the people was incredible. This was the biggest event of the year. After eating and singing for 16 straight hours, they would take a short nap and get right back up and go out and do it again. They never lost their vitality or their enjoyment. They just go right on until midnight on the thirteenth. Then, when the fourteenth of January hits, it's New Year's Day and Slavic is over. They put the star away in the church until the next year. It really was amazing to see how important Slavic is to the Russian Orthodox Yup'ik people. It was interesting to see how they took something that is Russian in tradition, and incorporated into it their own Yup'ik traditions.

Slavic is one of the biggest events for villagers in the whole year. They save their money and their food for this one event, and take great pride in it. All the women wear kerchiefs and dress up nicely in their dresses. They dress all the children up. You eat plenty of food for the spirits of the dead, and the people who have departed this earth before you. You eat food for them and you wish them well.

We Traveled the Road Less Traveled

By Don Elbert

It was June 14th 1998, one week before the longest day of the year. We summoned our pioneer spirit and drove through some of the wildest land in Alaska–theDalton Highway to Prudhoe Bay. My wife Elaine, her sister Sterlene, and I left Fairbanks and headed north in my 1978 school bus-converted-into-a-camper. I had previously decided that a $700 round trip Tour Bus ticket to Prudhoe Bay was beyond our reach; thus, my decision to drive the bus up north. My major concern was - *would this tired, old bus with a speedometer approaching 200,000 miles complete the trip?* Our friends John and Shirley didn't think so. We invited them along, but they decided to drive their own 4x4 Jeep Cherokee. John sells life insurance and he wanted to insure that he wouldn't be stranded in the Arctic if my bus broke down. Although they traveled separately, we all ate and slept in the bus. John's dry humor and Shirley's perky smile and witty comments added to the overall fun and enjoyment for all of us.

Years ago, in 1977-78, our son Dave and several of our friends worked up north during the pipeline days, and we had heard many bone-chilling tales and horror stories about the

North Slope Haul Road, which was later renamed the Dalton Highway.

Seventy-three miles out of Fairbanks, I, taking a leap of blind faith in my bus, turned off the Elliott Highway and began the 414-mile trip on the Dalton Highway. The bus purred along, while I said a silent prayer that it would keep purring as we traveled north, through wide-open country. We followed the world-famous oil pipeline as it slices through some of the most remote and spectacular raw land in Alaska. I envisioned a four-foot diameter, endless chrome caterpillar, crawling its way to Prudhoe Bay.

The natural scenery, forest, arctic mountains, rivers, tundra and coastal plains, awed us. We experienced the midnight sun along with some beautiful, sunny weather that changed to stormy and rainy, and back again as the miles rolled by.

The Dalton is a 28-foot-wide gravel road, built up three to six feet above the tundra with potholes, soft shoulders, and steep grades. Dust billowed when a trucker passed, blotting out the sky, and making it impossible to see the road, which scared us to death.

Our constant enemy was the relentless wind and dust. We were heavily rained on during several stretches of highway, and the rain turned the dust to mud on more than one occasion. Frequent showers created a layer of mud on our bug-splattered windshield. The windshield wipers were useless; they merely smeared the mud like a knife spreading peanut butter. The windshield washers hadn't worked in years, so I would stop and physically scrape this muck off the glass. Our windshield received a pelting of gravel when a trucker passed, and we end up with two chips in the glass.

The Dalton Highway was almost litter free, except for the carcasses along both sides of the road. No, not animal carcasses, but rubber carcasses. The remains of tires in various stages of blowouts, shredded and shattered.

Our 20-inch radial tires continued to bounce and roll over the various sizes and shapes of the rocks that we encountered. There were stretches of highway where it looked like all the sharp rocks were hand placed, pointing up. This rugged gravel thoroughfare eats up tires for lunch. I had two spares, recommended for anyone traveling this road, but prayed I wouldn't need them. One trucker that we talked to said he makes 96 trips over the Dalton a year, and spends $7,000 on tires alone.

Services were few and far between. Gas, food, telephone, lodging, and tire repair were available only at the Yukon River crossing (Mile 56), Coldfoot (Mile 175), and Deadhorse (Mile 414).

At Mile 56 we crossed the 2,290-foot-long bridge over the mighty Yukon River. The Yukon is the fifth largest river in North America, and a summer supply route to many inland villages. It begins in Canada, and flows over 1,900 miles before reaching the Bering Sea. We stopped so that Elaine and Sterlene could take pictures of this wide river flowing through the glacier-sculpted mountains. It was a scene that I drank in, wanting to capture it all in memory–a mental portrait that I could call up and enjoy on a cold, winter night. Elaine called our attention to a boat below, piled high with supplies and gear. Four Natives, three children, and one dog were preparing to depart for their fish camp.

We crossed the Arctic Circle at Mile 115, and stopped to take pictures and gloat on just being there. Our next stop was at Mile 175, a sparsely populated settlement called Coldfoot, for dinner that evening. Bad timing put us in the rear of a long buffet line of returning tourists. The food was worth the wait and gave us a chance to visit with some Outsiders, which is what Alaskans call people who don't live here.

After dinner we walked around town and through the well-stocked gift shop before an evening lecture started. A young girl with a cute smile and a ponytail that bounced when she walked told us about the pipeline, the tundra and the animals. She talked about enduring the winters: the cold, desolation, and loneliness, and how the population drops drastically, along with the temperature.

After the lecture I gassed up the bus, added a quart of oil, and checked the tires before we drove to a campground a few miles outside Coldfoot to spend the night. For convenience, I parked within walking distance of the lone outhouse. John pulled up behind my bus and joined us as we lit the burner, made a hot cup of cocoa, and added a pinch of brandy. We traded a few traveling experiences, compared animal sightings and shared derogatory remarks about the road. Then we all watched the sun dip low on the horizon, before climbing into our bunks and dozing off to the buzzing sound of a lone, seemingly harmless, mosquito.

An hour later, the silence of the night was shattered as that lone mosquito (apparently a scout) led the charge. An army of mosquitoes attacked and assaulted us as we lay sleeping. Shrill screams filled the bus, as we were jabbed awake by our assailants. I fell to the floor in an attempt to get away from them; but there was no escape, they were everywhere. Scared and in a panic, I knew we would have to battle for our lives. I reached over and poked John. We needed his help if we were going to survive. John, with a wild-man look of terror on his face, jumped up so fast that he hit his head on the top bunk. John's eyes crossed as blood began to trickle down his cheek. Several hundred mosquitoes pounced on him before he could even raise his arms in defense. Several minutes later John gasped, then slumped to the floor. I thought he was a goner. Looking skyward I offered a quick, silent prayer for him. The next thing I noticed was this beady- – eyed mosquito rising to the top of the swarm that encircled John's bleeding head. Its belly was swollen to the point of bursting, and it looked to be the size of a baby bottle filled with blood. This plump critter was flapping its wings wildly in an effort to take off, but he couldn't–he was too heavy. Then John stirred. He wasn't dead after all, and the anger and frustration was building up inside him. He wasn't about to give up. I thought I heard the theme to the movie "Rocky" in the background as he got his second wind. He was mad; he came up slashing and smashing. His fist hit dead center of that fat bug and I heard the loud spat as its belly exploded. Watching in amazement the color inside my bus changed in a fraction of a second! What was an aged, faded, school bus-yellow, became a freshly spray-painted, blood red.

I shot a quick glance over to see how my wife was surviving the onslaught. She wasn't doing well. She appeared to be in a state of shock. I grabbed her and shook her back to reality. Sterlene and Shirley pulled their heads out of their laps, and began regaining their composure. They joined us in our counterattack with the determination they had used in the past to conquer their strong-willed husbands. Each of us began flaying away, punching, swinging, kicking, anything to knock these bloodsuckers off our arms and legs, hands, and faces. We probably looked more like a grade school Karate class, than seasoned Alaska mosquito hunters. For the next 15 minutes it appeared that we had a chance. At least we were holding our own. But the mosquitoes swarmed back in superior numbers. More than a hundred of them were gnawing through my red flannel long johns. Then they all nailed me at once, and it hurt. The pain dropped me to my knees. It felt like being hit with birdshot from a dozen, double-barreled, 12-gauge shotguns all at the same time. Our energy and strength were diminishing fast. I looked high and low trying to figure out if they were funneling in through a hole they had gnawed in the side of the bus, or if they were breeding inside faster than we could smash them.

Suddenly the hair on my head bristled. I spotted this muscular mosquito who looked like he had been pumping iron. He had a fierce look in his piercing green eyes, and he was coming straight at me. He had the look of sheer determination, like Mike Tyson before a championship fight. He revved up his twin engines with antennae extended, and began lowering his multi-legged landing gears. His three-inch beak was fully erect for penetration. Once more doubling up my fists, I tried again and again to punch him in the beak using jabs, straight punches, hooks and uppercuts in an effort to bend his beak over and render him ineffective; but I missed every time. He was more agile than I was. I have survived, over the last five decades, all battles with large and cunning mosquitoes, but this giant coming at me now scared me to death. I turned, wanting to escape and that's when he hit. His beak felt like a dull nail being driven deep into my forearm. Excruciating pain shot up into my shoulder as he punctured the bone, I felt faint. I prayed, "God, help us."

Then I heard John scream, "We gotta get out of here."

It became clear that our lives were in grave danger. I yelled, "QUIET," in a desperate attempt to squelch the pandemonium and plan our retreat! The vote was quick and unanimous: we agreed to make a run for it. THEY could have the bus; we had to get away. Sterlene had grown pale and was faint from loss of blood, so we scurried to get her a large glass of tomato juice to replenish her system before our departure. John's bleeding had stopped. I figured our assailants had drained him dry. But no, John led the way running wildly for the only visible protection–the outhouse. Midway, I glanced back to see if THEY were following us. They were. It wasn't the bus they wanted. The midnight sunny sky had turned black with hordes of the flying killer, and it appeared they were on a mission to drain us dry!

Reaching the outhouse, John opened the door and the five of us piled into the cramped quarters of the one hole'er. I slammed the door tight behind us. Immediately, each of us began gasping for air. I thought it was because we were packed in like sardines and crushing life's breath out of each other, which we were. However, it soon became apparent that the pungent odor was the real culprit. It was foul! On a scale of 1 to 10, this was a 20! We gagged. The last patron had apparently given birth to something that didn't agree with him at all. I was holding my nose and gasping for air. The offensive aroma hung like a mist over a hot shower. Then I heard a barely audible cry from Sterlene, who had slumped to the floor, "Help me, please, I can't breathe," and her voice trailed off. At this point I figured our only chance of survival was to go back outside and battle the mosquitoes. I unlocked the door and tried to push it open, but it would only give an inch or so.

My eardrums nearly burst with the thunderous noise from the multitudes of mosquitoes flying formation outside. The steady pressure and resistance was a solid wall of mosquitoes holding the door and waiting for our exit. It was similar to a S.W.A.T. team awaiting a bank robber holed up in a phone booth. Through that narrow crack, I spotted the twin-engine fellow discussing strategy with his army. They were discussing the feasibility of carrying the outhouse back to their main camp where the really big ones were.

I turned around to assess our situation in time to hear Shirley losing her supper. Elaine and Sterlene were crying, gagging, and screaming for John and me to do something. I didn't have a gun or a club, and for the first time in my life I felt terribly inadequate. I didn't know what to do. My macho ego as a great Alaskan hunter and protector was shattered. I looked to John for help, but he had turned as white as fresh fallen snow. He wasn't going to be any help. My heart was beating so fast it sounded like a piston pounding in my chest. Sweat was flowing off me like a river. Holding my breath to keep the stench out, I could feel I was about to pass out. THEN, …then, I woke up.

WOW!-Still shaking, I got up, mopped the perspiration from my brow, made a pot of coffee, and sat pondering my nightmare. An hour later Elaine arose and made us a hearty breakfast of pancakes and sausages. Sterlene and Shirley didn't want to roll out of bed, but the aroma of that gourmet breakfast did the trick. While we lingered over the last cup of coffee, I calmed down enough to relate my frightful nightmare.

Then Shirley, showing no signs of mercy, and with a tinge of sleep deprivation, stated flatly: "I don't know when you had time to dream. Most of the night you were snoring so loud no self-respecting mosquito would get close." I could tell it was time to travel.

Ten miles out of Coldfoot, we turned into the old mining town of Wiseman, on the south flank of the Brooks Range. I wanted to see Wiseman because I had been there in 1957 when my dad had taken me sheep hunting. On that trip a bush pilot had flown us into town, as it was long before the highway was built.

Forty-one years later we walked through the small bush village and socialized with the locals. We visited their museum and spent an hour looking over the primitive mining equipment used to extract gold and reading about the intriguing history of Wiseman. Next, we stopped in their small, well-kept church, and we each knelt before the cross of Jesus to privately thank our Creator for His many blessings and this great land we live in ... and I prayed that the bus wouldn't let us down.

I took a long, last look at the mountains and felt a sense of pride and belonging, because 41 years ago, I was up there. I couldn't tell which mountain we had climbed, but it didn't matter, as we had climbed one.

Back on the road, my under-powered bus began climbing the mountains in the Brooks Range. The old vehicle slowed to 20 miles an hour on the steep grades. I was worried! My thoughts were: oh shucks, is this cantankerous bus going to quit on me? I looked for a place to leave the bus when it died, but it didn't die. It just kept plugging along at 20 mph all the way to the top, as though inspired by "The Little Train That Could."

Atigun Pass, at Mile 245, was an impressive sight–the

highest point of the pipeline at 4,739 feet. We stopped at a scenic point near the top and viewed the valleys and gorges that were all around us. Our eyes bulged as we took it all in. "What a view," John gasped, not wanting to leave. We contemplated which of these valleys had been shaped by angry rivers, and which ones gouged out by monster glaciers.

In the high mountain passes we encountered sheep by the hundreds on both sides of the road, and several sheep families crossing the road. A shaggy mother grabbed our attention as she nursed her two baby lambs beside the road. A little further on, we observed a big ram that looked as if he was trying to climb a vertical rock cliff. We watched him suck the water that seeped through a crack above him. The young sheep were fun to watch as they jumped and pranced, sure-footed on thin ledge rock formations.

Ice and snow packs several feet thick were common sights in the mountains, and on the riverbeds beside the road. We crossed numerous picturesque rivers and streams that cascaded down the mountains.

Along the highway there were several white crosses which served as a reminder to the living to slow down.

We dropped down out of the mountains, and the bus seemed to get its energy back, picking up speed. Next, we entered the North Slope, a treeless tundra that descends gently from the northern foothills of the Brooks Range to the Arctic Ocean. Here John's Jeep Cherokee had a flat tire, the victim of one of those sharp rocks that I described earlier.

Several flat rabbits appeared on the road. They were the snowshoe hares that thought the grass was greener on the other side of the road. Bad timing, trying to cross in front of a truck, had ended their hopping.

Through our bug-splattered windshield we watched a porcupine wobble along the side of the road. He wanted to cross, but was hesitant, knowing that danger lurked–not wanting to end up flat as his friend the rabbit.

We passed a Japanese walker pulling his two-wheel cart at Mile 270, just past Pump Station #4. He was averaging 15 miles a day, walking his way to Prudhoe Bay. With only 144 miles to go, he was on the downhill side of his 850-mile trek from Anchorage.

At mile 275, over a section of road built up six feet above the flat tundra, we came upon a guy standing in front of his van with a video camera. We stopped to ask what was so interesting. Pointing to the ditch, the man whispered, "Can't you see that grizzly? You folks better keep your eyes open."

From a sitting position in our bus we couldn't see the bear on the far side of the road; but when we stood up there he was, not 15 feet from us. He was a young bear with a beautiful, golden brown fur coat, munching grass and taking big bites, just like a cow. Our excitement grew as we watched him up close. This was a thrill because even life-long Alaskans don't often see bears. Sterlene, who had been riding with John and Shirley because my bus had been shaking her insides loose on the rough road, eased out of John's car and walked over to the side of the road near the bear to take pictures. I tried to hide the fear I felt for her as I quietly suggested that it was not a safe thing to do. With a deep blush, Sterlene sheepishly returned to the car. Several minutes later, the bear came up on the road beside my bus and walked on behind us for a short distance before dropping back down to the tundra in one lumbering movement. Elaine's voice was filled with excitement as she commented, "The wildlife alone makes this trip worth taking. I've seen more animals here than I've ever seen in Denali National Park." I agreed, and then remember thinking, *I hope the bear will be long gone by the time the Japanese walker gets here.*

The road was getting rougher as we proceeded north. My bus was shaking so bad I thought something would fall off. At the next stop, John noticed my tail pipe hanging loose, so we used a piece of bailing wire to hold it in place. A few miles up the road we waved a greeting to two bicyclists, who looked weary as they peddled at Mile 345, returning from Prudhoe Bay.

Further north at Mile 388, the terrain was still treeless and mostly flat. We encountered a large number of caribou from the Central Arctic herd, approximately 18,000 strong. They were thick, all over the tundra, with many on the road. We stopped several times to let them cross. Several caribou had large antlers that looked out of proportion to their bodies. I compared them to a cowboy wearing a hat with a 40-inch brim. Once we had to wait 20 minutes for the caribou to cross, and we enjoyed every second of it. Next, we saw a lone cow moose in a pond drinking water; she lifted her head as if to greet us and give her okay for us to pass.

Each of us could feel the chill in the air as we arrived that evening at the end of the road, a community called Deadhorse. We were just a few miles away from the Arctic Ocean and the Prudhoe Bay oil complex, but you can't drive there because of restrictions by the oil companies. If you want to see the ocean and the oil fields you are required to take the guided tour in a designated van.

In Deadhorse, we spent a cold, 40° night in the bus without any threat of mosquitoes. In the morning, I got up to start the bus and let it run for an hour to warm up the interior. We drank coffee and ate muffins until it was time to start the $50-per-person guided tour of the oil fields in Prudhoe Bay. I noticed the bus engine missing and shaking as I turned it off, but it was time to board the tour van. My thoughts: Is this old bus having a heart attack? Is it going to die on me?

It was a chilly, windy day and we all donned our parkas. Our first stop was at the Arctic Ocean where big solid chunks of ice were within 40 feet of shore. The tour was getting interesting, when our group of nine got a special thrill. Ben, a heavy-set member of our tour group from Michigan, informed us that he was going to take the "plunge." He stripped down to his swimming trunks right there in the van, then walked out and waded into the 32.7-degree water up to his thighs. He stopped and turned around to face us, revealing an open-mouthed, shocked expression. Ben grabbed his nose and laid down backward in the ice-cold water. I started to shiver in my parka just watching him. When he came up from the water, his face looked like he'd just seen a ghost.

Sputtering to catch his breath, he recovered and then showed us his fun nature by asking, "Anyone else like to join me?" No one did, so he hurried out of the cold water and returned to the van. Ben toweled off and put his clothes on over his wet swim trunks. He seemed no worse for wear, although he did mention that he thought his brain had iced up. Later we learned that this was prearranged, and our young guide Eric officially awarded Ben a certificate that stated the time and day of his plunge. Ben had a huge grin on his round face as he was pronounced an Official Member of the Arctic Alaska Polar Bear Club. Elaine, Sterlene, and Shirley came to a consensus: "No amount of money could entice me to take the plunge and lay down in that ice water!" John, on the other hand, and the bravest among us, boasted "If the price was right, I would do it!"

Next we saw the pipeline pig, not their mascot but the name of the plug-like intricate tool used to clean the inside of the pipe. Then, through a small hole cut in the insulation around the pipe, we took turns feeling the radiant heat from the 120-degree oil as it flowed south through the 48-inch pipe to Valdez.

The median temperature in the summer at Prudhoe is 40 degrees Fahrenheit and the wind was blowing, so no mosquitoes. Our guide, Eric, told us that he would rather be in Prudhoe in midwinter with 60°-below zero temperatures, than suffer through the occasional warm, summer days with no breeze and clouds of mosquitoes dive-bombing him without mercy. I could relate to his feeling by just recalling my nightmare.

Eric issued each of us a document certifying that on June 16, 1998, we had crossed the Arctic Circle. He also told us that the employees at Prudhoe work 84 hours a week, which isn't a problem because there is nothing else to do but eat and sleep.

We returned to the bus for soup and a ham sandwich before starting the trip home to Fairbanks. The bus started up, but was still missing on a couple of cylinders and had no power; it wouldn't go over 12 mph, even on flat ground. Again, I'm thinking: Please, bus, don't quit on me. Holding the gas pedal to the floor for the first half mile, we inched out of town. Then one flooded cylinder cleared, and a few minutes later the last cylinder fired up and we were on our way.

The return trip over the same road was just as exciting. We viewed new sights just because the lay of the land allowed us to see some things better going south. We stopped at Mile 115, the Arctic Circle Campgrounds for the night. In the morning John's car wouldn't start-the battery was dead. So I pulled my bus around and gave him a jump. We stopped next at the Yukon Bridge and again, John needed a jump. After this, John began parking his car facing my bus to make it easier.

I asked John what he was enjoying most about this trip. He grew several new wrinkles on his forehead, as he thought deeply before a pleasant smile broke the stern lines of his face. His soft answer, "One of the more beautiful parts of the trip for me was the treeless mountains that make up the Brooks Range." His voice was reverent as he went on, "They are massive, and their multicolored sides seemed to surround us as we drove through. When we were up on top, I could see forever and wherever I looked was another perfect, oh-so-beautiful mountain. I felt at peace with God and nature."

As we passed motorists and truckers on this sparsely-traveled highway, I would give a friendly wave to the passing vehicles. About 70% of them returned the greeting. I figured the other 30% felt more secure with both hands on the steering wheel and paying attention to their driving.

On Wednesday June 17th, we were 20 miles from home at 2:00 PM. We stopped at the Hill Top Restaurant for one of their famous omelets. I was working my way toward the center of my omelet, enjoying each bite, when I looked out the window to see the wonder of summer snow, falling in big flakes and covering the ground. I thought, "Snow is completely out of place as we are fast approaching the longest summer day of the year." I couldn't help thinking, "What is going on here? Has El Nino been around?" The snow didn't last long, though; it was melted by the time we departed the Hill Top.

As we pulled in the driveway at home, my lips proclaimed a silent prayer of thanks. The Dalton Highway had given my bus a licking, but it just kept on ticking. With only two new chips in the windshield the bus had made it back home. Our 20-inch radial tires held air over the rocky road, and nothing had shaken loose, except the tail pipe and Sterlene's insides.

We all looked forward to a warm shower, and it felt good to wash off the mosquito repellent mixed with Dalton dirt. It was a great trip and we were all glad we did it. The good news for me was that the bus didn't let us down, and the bailing wire held the tail pipe up. The final damage report from John's Jeep: ... one battery, one tire.

Two days after returning home I checked the bus. The engine was one quart low on oil, and the left rear inside dual tire was flat. Next, using a high-pressure hose, we washed the Dalton Highway dirt off the bus. We had accumulated enough mud and dirt to plant a rose garden! The bus was looking good again and had earned my respect. I thought to myself, *"I am sure proud of our bus; now, it's time to start thinking about our next journey somewhere else into Alaska's vastness."*

A Tale of Two Brothers

By Don Elbert

Alaska Versus Texas

Our father left my mother, brother Doug, and me back in Washington State in 1942. Dad, still reeling from the Great Depression, headed north to Alaska to find work in a new land, brimful of opportunity. Eventually, Dad settled on a 100-acre homestead site near Fairbanks, Alaska. He began clearing land, planting potatoes and farming vegetables. Five years passed. The farm grew, and my brother and me had grown big enough to help. During the summer of 1947 dad sent for us to come to Alaska to learn how to work, and over the next 11 years he taught us well.

Then dad lost his and the banks D-9 Tractor when it broke through the lake's ice. The potato market crashed, our spirits bottomed out, and the coldness of winter returned. Doug dreamed of living somewhere, anywhere warmer.

My fun-loving, intellectual 24-year-old younger brother Doug, didn't like ice, didn't like snow, and he surely didn't like freezing his fingers and toes in 40 below. He left Alaska back in 1958, during Territorial days, before Alaska became the 49th state. His parting words were: "I want to go where I won't have to wear long johns and a parka to keep from becoming an elongated ice cube."

Doug departed on the first fall day that the mercury dropped below zero, (*that's colder than inside a freezer).* That day, the sun spent the morning hiding below the horizon. As far as the eye could see, the land was painted white, and laid buried under four inches of freshly-fallen snow. Doug told dad and I, "I've had it with this cold, I'm outta here for good."

Doug roamed the lower 48 states looking for a temperate spot to live, where he could retire his parka and long johns. Doug's travels ended in Nacodoches, a quaint and tidy college town billed as the oldest town in Texas. Doug settled there, found work as an accountant, met and married a Texas beauty named Janith. To this day, he enjoys the warmth of Texas.

I, on the other hand, chose to stay in Alaska. I embraced the rugged lifestyle of the north and the cold challenges that this country has prepared for Alaskans eight months of the year. I met and married Elaine, the girl that put a sparkle in my eye and melted my heart. Through the years I worked as a heavy equipment mechanic, and I've been cold, really cold, more times than I can count.

Now 40 years later, in September of 1998, Elaine and I left Alaska on vacation. As the cold moved in, we moved out, just ahead of the snow. We followed the geese and the cranes and several of our snowbird friends who migrate south for the winter. We wanted to experience the good life, being warm and walking barefoot on the beaches, with sand tickling our toes. The only ice I wanted to see would come in a glass. Elaine was looking forward to soaking in a lake full of warm water, something bigger than our bathtub. We sought what we had been missing, solar heat. These happy images floated around in my head as we headed south to visit my brother.

As we drove across the border, the Texas sun welcomed us, then flooded my eyes with a brightness that nearly blinded me. Then the horror of our highway nightmare began. We almost got run over. The speed limit on the freeways is 70 miles an hour and that's in the slow lane. Most of the traffic, including the trucks, whizzed by at 75 and 80 mph. My old Honda had never been that fast in Alaska, and it took every bit of coaxing I could give, plus pushing the throttle one half inch past the floor boards to get up to speed.

I admit, Alaska has some need-of-repair roads. The permafrost is in the habit of heaving a stretch of highway like a cowboy cracking a whip. We've got potholes, chips, breaks, humps, and bumps; so my old Honda and I have learned to slow down and sneak up on a bad stretch of highway. Because of Alaska's road conditions, I had looked forward to the smooth ride on the super-concrete highways in Texas.

WRONG! At 70 mph, the breaks in the pavement every couple of car lengths shook three of my fillings loose! I felt like a cowboy riding a bucking bronco. The constant pounding that my car took shocked my shock absorbers and they quit absorbing. I thought about slowing down once, but one quick glance in the rear view mirror to see some trucker's BIG bumper about to make contact with my little Honda erased that idea. Texas truckers are way too friendly.

Texas roads are mostly litter free, except for the flattened armadillos and raccoons that didn't keep up with the 70-to-80-mph traffic. I'm sure they make quite a bump, but it wouldn't compare to what you feel in Alaska when a moose runs out in front of you! The driver considers himself lucky if his car is all that is totaled!

After polishing off a pint of nerve-calming medicine (taken for medicinal purposes only, of course...), we did arrive at my brother's white, paint-blistered cottage. The temperature was a way-too-hot 96 degrees.

We enjoyed our reunion and got reacquainted over the next few days, regaling each other with tales of the ups and downs in our lives over the past 40 years. Doug invited us to his favorite restaurant where we all ordered his special; steak and catfish. During dinner we were treated to a most enjoyable sideshow-three cockroaches racing across the floor to clean up under a table. I bet Doug a whole dollar on the bigger one with the protruding green eyes and long curly whiskers. That roach didn't win though; he stopped under a high chair, midway, to scarf up some french fries and devour the remains of a hot dog. Apparently he needed a little nourishment to continue. He was obviously unaware of the high stakes that I had placed on the race!

Leaving the restaurant, we waddled and burped back out to Doug's car, where I touched the hood for support and burned my hand. I told Doug, "Your hood is so hot, I could fry eggs on it." Doug thought a minute before answering, "No, you couldn't. I tried it once and by the time I got back out to the car, the eggs were all hard-boiled."

On the way home, Elaine asked Janith, "Are there any snakes in this area?" So Janith began telling Elaine about the big one that slithered up beside her while she was weeding the flowers – nearly caused her heart to stop. We practically had to pry Elaine out of the car after that bit of information.

Comparisons

After 40 years apart, I knew there would be many differences between my brother and myself, our lifestyles and experiences. Interestingly, we both ended up in the two largest states, but that's where the similarities stop!

I tell Doug, "You look different, your broad shoulders and narrow hips have swapped places. Your skin looks like a baked potato, cooked under the Texas sun." Then he walked away to the refrigerator for a Coke, and I say, "You resemble a tall tortoise walking on its hind legs. Furthermore, your legs look like a pair of parentheses and you don't even ride horses."

Doug remarked, "Ya'll look pale, like someone who hasn't seen the sun for some time. Your color resembles mashed potatoes. You look like a bear; the hair on your arms and legs has turned white, matching your head, and you've got more fur than a polar bear."

Doug said stuff like, "Ease up on life, slow down and watch the cactus growing."

Doug said I talked like a dam Yankee.

Doug's walk had changed with his years under the sun. He now walked with a lazy stroll claiming, "It is too hot to walk any faster." He usually shuffled around in light loafers, or sandals and thin socks.

I said, "I'm still in the habit of walking fast, from years of hurrying to get back inside to warm up." In Alaska, I wear mukluks or bunny boots and wool socks.

Doug said, "I wear thin clothing designed to keep me cool."

I reply, "Up north, I start with a pair of long johns before adding the outer layers, then don my parka and pulled-up hood."

"Your East Texas air is humid, hot and muggy; I can taste the water in it. I have to wring the sweat out of my shirt after a walk," I tell Doug.

"Your air in Fairbanks is too cold. It used to hurt my lungs just breathing," says Doug.

Doug said, "On a hot day I like iced tea, Pepsi Cola on ice, or a cold glass of water."

I reply, "On a cold day up north, I like a hot cup of coffee, cocoa, or tea to warm my chilled bones."

"My favorite dinner is a three-quarter inch, blood-rare beefsteak, with some catfish and shrimp on the side," says Doug.

I was watching Doug eat one rare steak, when I thought I heard it trying to breathe on its own. So I politely tell Doug, "I believe if you quit chewing on it, and add a few bandages to stop the bleeding, we could revive that one."

Doug shouted, "I don't think that was funny at all!"

"My favorite northern dish is a well-cooked moose hamburger, with some smoked salmon," I tell Doug.

"The view of the land is also remarkably different," I said, "Texas has a lot of flat land, with a few bumps and hills. Alaska has real mountain ranges topped off by Mount McKinley, the tallest peak in North America."

"Texas is full up with friendly people and lots of sunshine," says Doug.

I answered, "Alaska is vast, lots of room, and we're not all packed together like kernels on a corn cob."

Then Doug smiled with pride as he showed me his new Stetson, cowboy boots and silver spurs. So I ask Doug, "What lessons have you learned that you would like to pass on to us non cowboys."

Doug related his wisdom, learned the hard way.

"Don't breathe through your mouth when chewing snuff!"

"Don't step in fresh cow pies bare footed!"

"No matter what anyone tells you, don't believe it if it don't make sense!"

"Don't squat with your spurs on!"

I thanked Doug for passing on that helpful bit of info.

Hoping to get a heated debate started

I tell Doug, "I just heard Alaska is going to divide into two states, making your little old Texas the third largest state."

To which Doug squelched my conversational momentum when he replied: "If ya'll ever got a full week of good old Texas sunshine up there, it would melt all your snow and ice and you wouldn't have enough land left to plant a garden, let alone divide." He added, "If Alaska is so great, how come it's among the top three least populated states, huh? I think you must have frozen your brain to stay up there in the great 49th mistake."

I decided right then to change the subject, so we went for a walk.

Doug pointed with pride to a row of huge, tall magnolia trees that lined his lane, as we ducked under one for shade. The trunks must have measured 30 inches in diameter and the fully-leafed, thick, long branches tapered down from the top and reached 30 feet across, which remind me of a large lady wearing a long, full, brown-and-yellow-fall-colored skirt.

"Bet you don't have anything in Fairbanks to compare to

these beauties," Doug boasted.

I had to admit that trees don't grow when it's 40 below and the gnarly, stunted spruce around our cabin were not much to brag about.

Doug stated, "When it's hot out, we spend a lot of time indoors keeping cool."

And my reply, "When it's cold out, we spend a lot of time indoors keeping warm."

"In Texas, I hunt for deer and 'coon, and fish for catfish, bass, crappies, and perch" says Doug.

"In Alaska, I hunt for caribou and moose and fish for halibut, salmon, and grayling," says I.

I told Doug, "Driving on Texas roads scare me. Four-to-eight lanes, packed full of cars and big trucks, all intermingled and traveling well over a mile a minute, with a few *freeway cowboys* continuing to switch lanes to pick up yet more speed. And there I was, trying to avoid being run over, while being encased in this tightly woven traffic that is bumper to bumper. Talk about following too close, I never even walk that close behind someone, even if I like 'em, let alone while traveling at 75 mph." Then I mention that, "a few cowboys that whizzed by and seen a breath of air between me and the car in front, whipped right on in to fill the gap." I told Doug of suspecting they've been bucked off too many broncos. Doug confided to me, "I am one of them cowboy drivers, but I don't ride broncos."

I said, "In Alaska, I can still remember the two-lane dirt road in front of our cabin where you could count the cars that passed in a day on your fingers."

"Texas is too hot. It's like broiling in a slow-cook oven," I told Doug.

"Alaska is too cold, it's like walking into a giant freezer," Doug said.

"I start my car to cool it down before getting in," says Doug.

"I start my car to warm it up before getting in," I said.

I tell Doug, "One thing that bothers me in Alaska was having my glasses fog up when coming into the warm house from the cold outside." Well, it happened in Texas too; after getting out of his air-conditioned car into the 96-degree heat, my glasses fogged up again.

"Your air is too muggy, I feel like I'm in a sauna every time I go outside. The sweat pours out of me and I need a shower and a dry change of clothes after a short walk," I said.

"Quit complaining. If ya'll would take off that wool shirt and let those ice crystals in your bloodstream mclt, you will get used to it," Doug replied.

Then Doug tells us about it being so hot a month earlier that he saw a dog chasing a cat, and they were both walking.

"Wet your head down with water before going outside, it will help you keep cool," Doug says.

I told Doug, "If I did that in Alaska, my hair would break off."

The weather in Texas is very different. The week before we arrived, Texas had thunderstorms, flooding, and Hurricane Georges. We drove across the state and witnessed a part of the destruction, trees uprooted, buildings turned over, roofs blown off, and big signs torn down. The massive cleanup effort was in full progress, along with the damage assessment.

I said, "Your Texas weather goes from the heat inside your oven while baking bread, to throwing a fit and becoming downright violent."

Doug replies, "Your Fairbanks winters are just plain boring, freezing cold."

I said, "Texas rain is different the heavens open up, and rain comes down by the bucketful's."

Doug says, "You don't have normal rain in Alaska either, your rain comes down in snowflakes."

Our long awaited day on the beach arrived. We stopped at Padre Island and put on our swimsuits and walked out in the soft, hot sand. Both Elaine and I enjoyed the foot-massaging sensation of the sand oozing between our toes. Stepping out into the pleasant water was a warm comfort to my aching back, and it brought a heavenly smile to my wife's face. Later, we stretched out on our beach towels hoping to absorb a suntan like my brother had. It wasn't long before I began feeling like a cooked goose.

Just then, Doug glanced over and noticed how red Elaine and I had turned. "Ya'll look like a couple of boiled lobsters," he shouted with alarm. We headed for cover. In the days and weeks that followed, I never knew if we had first or second degree burns, but as the pain slowly receded, we both shed several layers of skin and wore our fingernails down to the nubbins itching and scratching.

Three Weeks Later

I asked Doug, "Now that we are reaching our twilight years, was Texas a good choice? Have you been happy here?" Doug's answer, "Yup, Texas has been good to me and I still like being warm."

I replied, "I still like Alaska, and I don't like being too hot. I can't take off enough clothes in Texas to be cool.

However, up north I could put on enough to stay warm most of the time. I guess it all depends on your mindset and what you're willing to put up with."

Doug and I did agree on what may be the ultimate in experiencing good weather. To spend the Texas hot summers in Alaska, and spend Alaska cold winters in Texas. Sharing the best weather offered by these two great states is as good weather wise as life can get here on earth.

The weeks flew by and time came for Elaine and I to head back to Alaska, where we could cool off. As we said good-byes and parted company, I felt a deep sadness come over me. I love my brother, and I have missed him over the long years apart. However, I think I've had enough of that solar heat to last me another 40 years.

Doug and I have adapted well to our chosen homeland. After our many talks, I know in my heart that we each hold firmly to our belief that, "I had made the better choice!"

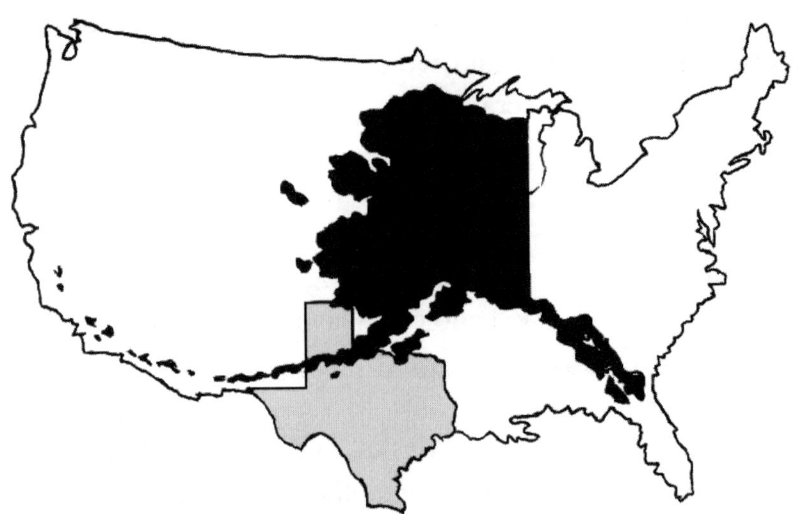

Alaska Has Captivated Our Hearts

I had just met this pleasant, older lady in Phoenix, Arizona, and in the course of our brief conversation, noticing my paleness, she asked, "Where are you from?" I replied, "I'm from Alaska." A shocked expression crossed her deeply tanned and wrinkled face, and in all seriousness she asked "Why do you choose to live in a frozen land, under a blankets of snow all year?"

Fighting back a tinge of anger at her audacity, I was tempted to ask her why she chose to live in Phoenix where the sun can melt the paint off your car, but thought better of it. But, her question bothered me–a lot. It kept bouncing around in my mind like a melody that won't leave you alone. So I asked friends and neighbors how and why they came and stayed in Alaska. -- Don Elbert

Just Married and Paul Says, "To Alaska"

By Christa Crisman

I have lived in Fairbanks now for 40 years and I want to tell you why I love Alaska. I grew up in Prussia, Germany during the nightmare and the reality of World War II. One dreadful night when I was 14, terror struck; bombs took away most everything I knew and loved.

My mother, sister, and I were left alone and scared. All we had was each other, but we survived. After the war ended, I chanced to meet Paul, a handsome young American who was visiting Germany, and we fell in love. Communicating was a problem at first; I had learned some English in school, but during the war I didn't have much schooling.

Paul talked a lot about going to Alaska. I had no idea how far Alaska was, so he showed me. Oh, he was so very clever. He showed me a little map and he said, "Look at this. Here is Germany and here is Alaska." I put my thumb on Germany and my finger on Alaska; it looked about three centimeters. And I said, "That's not far, I could easily come back. Sure, yes!" He said, "You want to marry me?" And I said, "Sure." So we were married and Paul said, "To Alaska."

We moved to Fairbanks, and Paul worked and we saved. To me the biggest thing was to get a piece of ground first. We rented for eight years, and we saved every penny to get our own land. We were lucky to find our property here on Farmer's Loop, and we built our home and raised our family on our own piece of ground. Over the years we've had gardens, greenhouses, horses, dogs-name it, we had it. To me, this piece of ground here means more than anything! The people have been just beautiful, charitable, and generous. It's going to be awfully hard–now that I'm getting old, and we can't take care of our little homestead here–to give it up and move. It's going to be my saddest day. I don't ever want to leave Alaska.

My Love Affair with Alaska

By Dorothy Flora

I drove the Al-Can Highway on my first visit to Alaska in 1974, and I vowed I would never return! I was too upset about the drive up here, which was not a normal trip. Three flat tires, a shattered windshield, and the jarring effect of the road raised havoc with my temperament. My mud-splattered truck/ camper, and dozens of insect bites were no instruments of fun.

But I did return 24 years later, for a two-week visit. I flew into Fairbanks on a bright summer day in 1994. I was greeted with an entirely new focus. With my mind off the tortures of the Highway, I was able to notice the beautiful flowers growing everywhere, and also that the sky was bluer here.

The potatoes and cabbage tasted so good, as did everything else they grew here. But best of all, there was so much space! When my two weeks were over, I felt such sadness in leaving. I couldn't explain it.

In 1995, I began spending my summers here, working at my daughter's newly-acquired greenhouse where we grew tomatoes, cucumbers, and roses for sale in the local markets. My love affair with Alaska had begun! How the locals appreciated the Alaska-grown produce! With such fierce pride, they willingly paid twice and three times the amounts they would pay for the same produce flown in.

I learned more about these locals. Most had come from somewhere else, but now they were Alaskans. They liked each other not because of wealth, status, education, etc., but because of their character. People wave to passers-by, even if they don't know them; it's a friendliness that I had never seen in Washington or Oregon. When my car broke down on the road, I was helped by total strangers, without any feeling of apprehensiveness. I simply felt safe.

In the midst of this huge vastness, there is an almost surprising abundance of artistic talent, and support for that talent. It's almost like a family pride in what one of the children has accomplished-even I feel it.

Most of what I have seen and experienced here has been goodness and happiness. This past May, I left a very comfortable life and lovely home to move to Fairbanks.

My house here is not so luxurious, I share it with my daughter and four dogs (unheard of in Oregon), and my car is always dirty. But I have found something far more valuable–absolute peace of mind; and everyone has made me feel so welcome!

Why I Choose Alaska

By Joyce Clark

My friends and family Outside do not understand why I stay here. They say the cold and long nights would be depressing and uncomfortable.

I flew into Alaska on Wien Air 17 years ago looking for a bigger slice of independence and freedom. I lived on the Kenai Peninsula for five years; left in 1986 to go Outside for college, and returned with a teaching degree in 1989. I substitute-taught at all grade levels and all subjects for two years, and then moved to Fairbanks. My main reason for moving to Fairbanks was the accessibility of transportation and a larger job market. I have worked as a receptionist for the last seven years.

I can only say that I like it here! I like the mountains with their snow covered aretes, the tors that reach toward the stars. I like the vast expanse of the tundra that seems to go on forever. I like the sunsets, when the sky turns pink with tinges of orange against a cloud-strewn sky.

In the fall, I like the way the aspen and birch turn a bronze-gold, and the way straggly cedars provide a dark contrast. I like seeing the moose foraging by the road, and how the eagles soar and come to rest in the crown of a tree. Wintertime, I like the long nights when the stars are out, and the Aurora dances against the canopy of the night. Summertime, I like the long days when the sun is high at midnight and you can fish, or garden, or play ball, or simply sit on your terrace or lawn and enjoy the sun. I like the fresh rawness that still exists here, the expectation of being able to find and accomplish a dream.

I like the way Alaskans treat their elders–note, I said elders, not senior citizens! The term "elders" denotes a deeper respect. I like that. We are considered assets, not debits! Treasures to be mined, holders of tradition and truth; people to be valued.

I like the people. A mix of different cultures, different races, and most of us living together as friends, learning from one another.

Life is hard, they say here on the last frontier, and that is good! The difficulty of living, of surviving, is what draws us together as a community. It is what helps us work together to solve our problems.

Alaska ~ The Great Land

By Bill Hamilton

Alaska is truly a land flowing with milk and honey. In fact, Alaska goes far beyond this beautiful figure of speech, and has become a land flowing with oil, fortune seekers, and some of the very finest people on earth. Most anybody who understands this vast region would rather be an orphan in Alaska than quintuplets in any other state in the nation.

You must travel Alaska not only during summer, when there is teeming plant life in endless shades of green; or in winter when the land seems cold and lifeless, as if covered with a grave cloth of spotless white–and bears and motorboats are in hibernation. Travel also in the spring, when a warm drizzle brings relief to the ice-choked streams, and each little rivulet goes laughing and gurgling down the gentle slopes toward the turquoise sea; spring, when plants are aroused from their silent slumber. And in the fall, when everything is arrayed in the gorgeous tints and hues of Indian Summer, and all the motley colors of mid-autumn fade away in the light of a late September moon. Then, and only then will you know Alaska as it is.

Alaska is a great, big, beautiful slice of the Master's handiwork. I am proud of every sprig of her plant life, every ounce of her mineral wealth, every fish swimming in her streams, every animal treading on her tundra, every snowflake on her mountain tops, and every drop of oil deep down in her innards. And even if Alaska is not the greatest state in our wonderful nation, it is at least one state in the greatest nation on earth, America...and that's a lot to be thankful for.

Certainly, I am proud to live in Alaska...but you will

never thoroughly appreciate the big state until you've seen an arctic gale and witnessed untold tons of floating ice lunge like a bull moose against a rocky shoreline … or a blast of red hot cinders spout skyward from a troubled spot in the Valley of Ten Thousands Smokes…or an avalanche of frozen snow rumble wildly down a windswept mountainside…or a panic-stricken moose calf race madly through the puddle-studded muskegs with a pack of half-starved wolves grabbing at his heels…or a herd of white whales (belugas) churn the brine, while slashing savagely through a school of scampering herring…or the breathtaking aurora dance in the firmament, painting a primrose haze on the spacious canvas of purple polar sky…or a wounded grizzly charge blindly through the tangled underbrush with far more than a quizzical expression on his dew-dampened face. A heavy application of seal oil is needed to hold down one's hair at times like these.

Alaska is not a far-away wasteland of eternal ice and snow. Instead, to those who know its incomparable beauty and richness, Alaska truly is the "World's Greatest Wonderland."

We Came to Visit and Fell in Love with Alaska

By Lorene Finger

We came from the beautiful state of Colorado to visit Alaska, and fell in love with the people and the spirit of adventure. My husband and I were both teachers and we accepted a teaching position out in the bush in Unalakleet 35 years ago. We later moved to Fairbanks, and my husband built our first house. The weather has never been a problem; we've had picnics outside in 20° below zero and loved the challenge.

I Yearned to see Alaska

By Suzanne S. Hall

I first became conscious of the word "Alaska," in 1930, back in Pennsylvania. My first grade teacher told us intriguing stories about this far away land and its people, and I was fascinated. By the time I was a high school senior I had researched enough at the library to peak that interest, and to think that I would like to live there. Interrupting my studies of architecture at Carnegie Tech in Pittsburgh, I found my way to Fairbanks in July 1946–my initial adventure. Perhaps because I had anticipated coming to Alaska for so long, I was captivated immediately.

What do I love about Alaska?

I welcome the diversity, friendliness, and graciousness of its people where individuality is expected and cherished. A spirit of exploration exists that is demanded by the beauty of the land and its seasons. I've become part of a pioneer family of integrity, awareness, and appreciation of Alaska's history.

I enjoy the simple pleasures of berry-picking, coffee on tailing pile campfires, swimming in gravel pits. Down to 40 degrees below zero, I muffled our brood of children for daily walks and returned home with a renewed appreciation for our warm and snug log house. To me, winter is a delight. My children grew up learning independence, necessitated by lifestyles and the environment. Tears of joy flow when I hear our well-traveled grandchildren singing the Alaska Flag Song. What do I love about Alaska? It seems to draw me closer to God.

I'm a Survivor

By Bob Tyler

I was young and restless, fresh out of the Navy, and fed up with the hot weather in the South. Sensing my uneasiness, my uncle told me, "Go to Alaska and *cool-off*." I took his advice, arriving in Fairbanks, January 2, 1961. When I stepped off the plane I was greeted with 54 degrees below zero temperature. I went into shock. The first few seconds gave me all the *cooling-off* I wanted. I tried to get right back on that plane, but I didn't have a ticket.

In the two weeks that followed, it was dark most of the time. The severe cold saturated everything that wasn't heated, making it difficult to get around. I thought, I must have been out of my mind! I asked myself, "Why did you trade the warm climate back home for these freezing temperatures?" I couldn't answer that question, but I did want to wring my uncle's neck. Two more weeks went by and that was enough,

I wanted out of this icebox. I just needed a job to make the money for a plane ticket.

The next day my life received a ray of hope, I landed a job at Ft. Wainwright and went to work at the Commissary. For transportation, I either took the bus to work or caught a ride with a co-worker named Mr. Finney. While working at the Commissary, I met Nell, the love of my life and future wife. She's the reason I delayed buying that plane ticket out of town, and as the weeks flew by, the outside temperature and my disposition warmed up.

Three months later, spring arrived, the sun returned and the snow and ice melted. This revealed potholes and turned sections of the roads to mud. One day coming home from work, Mr. Finney's car sunk right down to the axle, and we had to call a wrecker. There were only five or six paved streets in Fairbanks at that time.

In June I bought myself a used pickup truck to get to work. The following winter of 1961-62, the temperature plunged to 78° below zero for three weeks. That's when I learned how to survive the cold. I bought a winter parka and matching warm clothing. To prevent my truck from becoming a big ice cube, I installed an electric engine heater, a battery blanket, and an interior heater. I did experience several flat tires–at that extreme cold temperature synthetic rubber tires have trouble holding air. One morning I came out of my apartment early to start my truck for its routine ten minute warm up before going to work. My truck leaned to the left, indicating I had another flat tire. I got my jack, loosened the bolts, removed the flat and went to get my spare. When I rolled the spare out of the back of my pickup, it dropped to the ground, but it didn't bounce, it shattered into pieces. I was so mad I cussed the weather and kicked the rim, which only further numbed my cold toes. I took a cab to work that day.

Now, looking back over my 38 years of residence, I can say I love Alaska and would never want to live anywhere else. I've become a survivor. I've traveled over Alaska's giant mountains, looked down and seen the beauty of the weaving rivers and streams. I've looked up and seen wildflowers and the different shades of vegetation on the ridges. While watching the sunrises and sunsets in these areas, my mind reflects back to the Psalms in the Bible of how God took his hands and shaped the valleys. I remember occasions on mountaintops where I would just close my eyes and thank the Creator who put all this awesome beauty together for all of us to enjoy.

Alaska does indeed have some tough winters, but together Nell and I have survived'em. As a hobby I have recorded temperatures since 1962. Alaskans love to talk about how cold it is, and I keep records. I've only been out of Alaska once and that was for two weeks in 1985, and I got homesick and couldn't wait to get back. When I crossed the Canadian border, coming back into Alaska I felt peace come over me. Maybe this sounds strange, but Alaska just grew inside of me. It took root and I knew this is where I wanted to be; this is my home.

On a Quiet Day

By Paul Elbert

The good feel of the wide-open spaces with room to breathe is a big reason why I chose Alaska. I am a farmer, and in the long, daylight hours of summer I truly enjoy watching my farm produce grow. Potatoes so big I couldn't get three into an apple box. Giant radishes gone from seed to maturity in 28 days. On a quiet day, when I stand very still, I really believe that I can hear my cabbages growing.

Alaskan Facts & Figures

Alaska is a geographical phenomena: active volcanoes, frozen glaciers, hot springs, permafrost, the deepest lakes and the highest mountain in the Western Hemisphere.

Alaska Was ALAXSXAQ

The name for the 49th state comes from the Native Aleut language and the name was Alaxsxaq. The Russians simplified it to "Alyeska" and the Americans reduced it to "Alaska." The Aleut word for their homeland literally means "where the sea waves break upon themselves."

Captain Vitus Bering of the Russian Navy first sighted Alaska in 1741, proving that Asia and North America were not connected.

Alaska-the Best Deal by Far

The bulk of Alaska is owned and managed by the federal government, which purchased Alaska from Russia in 1867. (This purchase for $7,200,000-or less than two cents an acre-was by far the best bargain of any land purchase deal in U.S. history.) The remaining area of Alaska, which is owned by private individuals and Native corporations, is about the same size as the area of Michigan.

How Big is Alaska?

- Alaska covers 375,296,000 acres or 586,412 square miles.
- Its greatest distances: east-west - 2,400 miles
- Its greatest distances: north-south - 1,420 miles
- Alaska has 33,904 miles of shoreline - that's 33% of America's total shoreline.
- Seventeen of the highest mountain peaks in the U.S. are in Alaska.

Alaska is the Size of:

You can fit ____________ in one Alaska
your state

11 - Alabamas
5 - Arizonas
11 - Arkansas'
3 - Californias
6 - Colorados
114 - Connecticuts
277 - Delawares
10 - Floridas
10 - Georgias
88 - Hawaiis
7 - Idahos
10 - Illinois'
16 - Indianas
10 - Iowas
7 - Kansas'
14 - Kentuckys
12 - Louisianas
17 - Maines
54 - Marylands
69 - Massachusetts'
10 - Michigans
7 - Minnesotas
12 - Mississippis
8 - Missouris
4 - Montanas
7 - Nebraskas
5 - Nevadas
61 - New Hampshires
73 - New Jerseys
5 - New Mexicos
12 - New Yorks
11 - North Carolinas
8 - North Dakotas
14 - Ohios
8 - Oklahomas
6 - Oregons
13 - Pennsylvanias
470 - Rhode Islands
18 - South Carolinas
7 - South Dakotas
14 - Tennessees
2 - Texas'
7 - Utahs
59 - Vermonts
14 - Virginias
8 - Washingtons
24 - West Virginias
10 - Wisconsins
6 - Wyomings

- ☛ In 1880, Alaska's population was 33,426. By 1994, its population had grown to over 500,000 residents, making Alaska the third least-populated state. By 1998, Alaskan population had grown to over 615,900 residents.
- ☛ Alaska has a population density of slightly more than one person per square mile.
- ☛ Caribou outnumber people in Alaska almost two to one.
- ☛ The moose was by far the mammal of choice to become the state's official land mammal of Alaska.
- ☛ The Alaska state bird is the ptarmigan, not the mosquito.
- ☛ There is a town in Alaska named Chicken because the town fathers couldn't spell ptarmigan. Gold is what attracted the early miners to Chicken. The road to Chicken is only open during the five summer months, (no snow plowing services).
- ☛ The word Eskimo is derived from a Native American word meaning "Eaters of Raw Meat."
- ☛ More earthquakes occur in Alaska than in any other state in the U.S. The Alaska Earthquake Information Center detects 70 to 120 earthquakes in Alaska every week. Three of the 10 largest earthquakes recorded in the world occurred in Alaska. The magnitude 9.2 earthquake that occurred in south–central Alaska, March 27, 1964 was the second largest earthquake ever recorded. This earthquake released 63 times as much energy as the largest recorded earthquake in California.
- ☛ Northern Lights–the Aurora Borealis, has a curtain-like shape, and the altitude of its lower edge is 60 or 70 miles, about ten times higher than a jet aircraft flies. Fairbanks, Alaska is a good place for Aurora watching. The Auroral intensity varies from night to night, with the best viewing

usually from late evening through the early morning hours, from September through April.

- ☛ Denali National Park is slightly larger than Massachusetts. Inside its boundaries is Mount McKinley, the highest mountain on the North American continent. Its south peak is 20,320 feet high.
- ☛ Alaska waters produce the largest salmon runs in the world.
- ☛ The king, or Chinook, female salmon can produce from 4,000 to 14,000 eggs. And then it dies.
- ☛ Yukon River King salmon has the highest protein in the world.
- ☛ "Eulachon" (or hooligan) are smelt. They are also known as candle fish, because these oily little fish were traditionally used as a candle when dried and fitted with a wick.
- ☛ The three bodies of water that make up Alaska's 33,904 miles of coastline are the Arctic Ocean, Pacific Ocean and the Bering Sea.
- ☛ The first Becoming an Outdoors-Woman clinic offered in Alaska had more than 100 women gathered from all over the state in December 1995, at Chena Hot Springs Resort to learn how to grunt a moose love call.
- ☛ Alaska's major industries are oil, fishing, mining, and tourism.
- ☛ The record snowfall in a season was 974.5 inches at Thompson Pass, near Valdez, during the winter of 1952-53. The record snowfall in 24 hours was 62 inches, at Thompson Pass in December 1955.
- ☛ The record low temperature was minus 80 degrees Fahrenheit at Prospect Creek Camp, in the Interior on

January 23, 1971, though colder temperatures have occurred without official verification.

- ☛ "North Pole" was the name selected over "Mosquito Junction" and "Moose Crossing" for the city just 12 miles south of Fairbanks.
- ☛ The city of Fairbanks was named in honor of Charles W. Fairbanks, vice president of the United States (1905-1909). He never set foot in Alaska.
- ☛ Alaska's first gold discovery was in 1848 by a Russian explorer.
- ☛ The largest gold nugget ever found in Alaska was discovered on September 29, 1903 in Nome. The nugget, weighing 155 troy ounces, was seven inches long, four inches wide, and two inches thick.

The Facts from Prudhoe Bay

- ☛ The 800-mile Trans-Alaska Pipeline is 48 inches in diameter and cost about $8 billion dollars.
- ☛ The pipeline crosses 800 rivers and streams and three mountain ranges.
- ☛ In early 1997, the pipeline was handling about 1.4 million barrels of oil, condensate, and natural gas liquids per day. It takes about six days, traveling at just over five and one-half mph for the oil to make the trip to Valdez.
- ☛ One barrel of oil equals 42 gallons.
- ☛ The longest day at Prudhoe Bay is 63 days, 23 hours, 40 minutes–from May 20 to July 22.
- ☛ The longest night at Prudhoe Bay is 54 days, 22 hours, 51 minutes–from November 24 to January 18.
- ☛ The shortest day at Prudhoe Bay is 1 hour, 3 minutes on November 24.

- ☛ The shortest night at Prudhoe Bay is 26 minutes on May 19 and 20.
- ☛ The highest temperature recorded at Prudhoe was 83 degrees F., June 21, 1989.
- ☛ The lowest temperature at Prudhoe, minus 62 degrees F., was on January 27, 1989.
- ☛ The highest wind speed, 109 MPH on February 25, 1989.
- ☛ The official low chill factor was recorded February 28, 1989. It was minus 54 degrees with 36 MPH winds, which gave us a chill factor of minus 135 degrees F.

- Motorists Tip -

Un-plug your car before driving away from the house.

The Harsh Winters

Alaskans learn that:

… Freeze-up is when the temperature drops below 32 degrees and stays there. Most liquids left out will freeze, and stay frozen, until the spring temperatures thaw them.

... You don't need a freezer for six months of the year. The whole outside is frozen.

... It's best to tie up your sled dogs, and plug in your car for the night.

... Your car rolls out in the morning (if you can get it started), with what feels like four flat tires.

... The term "mean temperature" in Alaska can be downright cruel.

... You are frostbitten when your hands, face, ears, nose, or toes go numb and turn white. Some of us Alaskans get a touch of frostbite every winter.

… Sourdoughs enjoy outdoor hot springs even at 40 degrees below zero. They also know that wet hair freezes and breaks off at that temperature and if they break off enough hair, they won't need a haircut.

... A warming trend is when the temperature rises from minus 60 degrees to minus 40 degrees.

... You sometimes strain to see through the long, dark winter days and nights using lanterns and candles.

... Ice fog (frozen water vapor) can be extremely hazardous. You just can't see far. You lose track of where you are, what's in front of you, and what direction you are going.

... A blanket of snow covers most of Alaska for six or seven months of the year. The good news is that it helps keep the dust down, and the land becomes a winter wonderland!

... Ice worms really do exist. Ice worms are small, thin, segmented black worms, about one inch long. They live on glaciers.

... The largest ice worm in the world comes out once a year in February, in the Iceworm Festival in the town of Cordova. A 150-foot-long, multi-legged "Iceworm" marches in a parade down the main street.

... You get warm three times if you cut your own firewood: cutting it, hauling it, and burning it.

... Some sourdoughs have had to seek a cure for a case of cabin fever. Cabin fever is having the blahs, a state of mind blamed on being closed up inside a small cabin too long, because it is too cold and dark to go outside.

... Many sourdoughs and miners wear their woolly long johns year round; in the winter to keep warm, and in the summer to keep cool by the cooling effect of the evaporation of perspiration.

... An "arctic entry" is a storm porch, and its purpose is to help keep the arctic cold from entering.

... Alaska is the home of "Old Man Winter."

... Eskimo ice cream is a whipped mixture of berries, seal oil and snow. It has its own distinct flavor, and is still not available at Baskin Robbins.

... You can eat muktuk (also known as whale blubber,) a favorite of the Eskimos and, surprisingly, learn to like it.

... Originally, mukluks were boots made of the skins of a mukluk. "Mukluk" is the Yup'ik Eskimo word for the bearded seal.

... From Fairbanks you go south to the city of North Pole to see Santa, who lives on Santa Claus Lane.

The Long-Awaited Summers

Alaskans learn that:

… After the long winter comes breakup, when the sun and the temperatures rise to melt the snow and ice. It's springtime in Alaska.

... You have experienced permafrost when the sun warms the land, the frost melts under your cabin, and your cabin tilts.

... June and July are true mosquito months.

... Male mosquitoes are vegetarians. That's the good news, but female mosquitoes insert a stinger in you and suck blood; that's the bad news.

... If you have the fortitude and patience, you can watch a mosquito on your arm fill up like an oil tanker in Valdez.

... If your average sourdough had as many mosquito stingers sticking out of him as have been stuck in him over the years, he would look more like a porcupine.

... The favorite perfume of Alaskans is insect repellent. The bad news is that it's become a favorite of the mosquitoes also.

... The life span of a mosquito is about six weeks, less if swatted.

... It is not easy to walk without falling on the spongy tundra, called muskeg. It's a little like trying to walk on top of a bunch of basketballs.

... You can use an "ulu" knife for all your cutting needs. But be careful, they're sharp.
... To do the knuckle-hop and the ear-pull, a favorite sport of the Alaska natives, it is best to prepare for a pain-endurance contest.
... The Eskimo blanket toss was the forerunner of the modern-day trampoline, and was originally used to allow Eskimo hunters to get high enough to spot game.
... You hear someone talking about going "Outside," and you wonder if they're talking about the lower 48, or just going to the outhouse.
... Squaw candy is a name for dried strips of salmon, a traditional native snack. Even the bears love it.
... Many sourdoughs have been plagued with a serious case of **GOLD FEVER**. This ailment is a passion that drives them to the creeks, with gold pan in hand, in the everlasting search for the next flake of gold. The finding of gold has started many a stampede.
... A poke is a leather bag in which miners carry their gold. Lucky miners use wheelbarrows.
... Gold-bearing earth is shoveled into a sluice box. Gold is separated from the earth by controlling the amount of water running through the trough. It sure beats panning!
... "Cleanup" is recovering the gold from the bottom of your sluice box.
... The miners' dream and goal in life is to find the mother lode, the rich source of gold.
... Many prospectors came to Alaska with more gold in their teeth, or on their watchband, than they ever found in their prospecting.
... A cache is a place to store food above ground, safe from critters and frozen all winter.

… Many Alaskans pick wild blueberries and cranberries to store up for the winter, just like the bears do.

... A "sheefish" is not necessarily a she. Could be a male sheefish.

... The "trail of 42"–the Alcan, which was constructed in 1942-43, has progressed from a trail to the paved Alaska Highway of today.

... You can enjoy the all-Alaska sport of dodging potholes, dips, and frost heaves on our roads and streets. Be advised however: they are "strategically placed," so you can't miss them all.

... Many sourdoughs prefer sourdough pancakes to buttermilk pancakes.

... You can watch a midnight sun baseball game in Fairbanks, with no artificial lights.

... In the fall of the year, the geese gather and head south to warmer weather.

... You also notice the "snow birds" flocking in the fall. They are the wiser Alaskans who can afford to head south for the winter. Sourdoughs scoff at snowbirds, until they can become one.

... The state motto is "North to the Future." The snowbird's motto is "south for the winter!"

Alaska's Awesome Wildlife

Polar bears are symbolic of the Arctic. These great white bears are a mixture of beauty and power. They live on drifting ice and swim in icy water. Their main prey is seals. A polar bear in good shape needs about 200 pounds of seal meat a day. These bears can run 35 mph, and are the only bears that have hair on the soles of their feet. It is common for a mother polar bear to deliver two tiny cubs weighing 1 to 1.5 pounds each. Due to mother's rich milk, these cubs can weigh 25 pounds by the time they leave the den in the spring.

Brown and grizzly bears are considered to be the same awesome creatures. The brown bears live on the coast, and the grizzly bears live in the interior. The Kodiak brown bears are the largest bears in the world. The reason they grow so large is that they eat so well during the salmon run. Beware of bears because they are usually looking for something to eat. Bears are curious, intelligent, and potentially dangerous animals.

Muskox are stocky, long-haired mammals. Mature bulls stand about five feet at the shoulder and weigh 600-to-800 pounds. Roughly 2,000-to-3,000 muskoxen live in Alaska. During the rut, battles between bull muskoxen, are spectacular and violent contests. Bulls charge one another at top speed from distances of 50 yards or more, and collide squarely on the horn bases. Although muskoxen may appear to be clumsy and slow, they can move with surprising agility and speed. The sound of the impact can often be heard a mile away. A battle may include 20 clashes.

The name "muskox" is misleading. These animals do not smell musky and are not oxen. They are best known for their long hair and fine underwool called "qiviut." Qiviut (kiv-ee-et) has been called the “Golden Fleece of the Arctic”–the rarest fiber in the world, it makes the warmest, soft sweaters, hats, scarves, and mittens.

Caribou are stout members of the deer family, with concave hoofs that spread widely to support the animal in snow and soft tundra. The weight of adult bulls averages 375 pounds; females average 200 pounds. Biologists estimate that there are close to a million caribou in Alaska.

In the spring, the females migrate to the calving grounds. In late May or early June, a single calf is born; twins are very rare. Newborn calves weigh about 15 pounds and usually double their weight in 20 days. They can walk within an hour of birth, and after a few days can outrun a person and swim across lakes and rivers. Like most herd animals, caribou must keep moving to find adequate food.

The caribou and the reindeer are considered to be the same species. In Alaska and Canada the domestic forms are called reindeer. Most adult male caribou and moose are "bald" (shed their antlers) by January after the rut. The female caribou shed theirs in the spring. The difference between antlers and horns is that antlers are shed each year and a new set is grown; horns are permanent.

Moose are the largest member of the deer family. Full-grown males stand six feet tall at the shoulders and weigh from 1,200-to-1,600 pounds, when in prime condition. Moose are long-legged and heavy bodied with a drooping nose, a "bell" or dewlap under the chin, and a small tail. Bulls can carry antlers that weigh up to 100 pounds, and measure up to 72 inches in width.

Newborn calves weigh 28-to-35 pounds, and within five months grow to more than 300 pounds. Moose are eating machines. During the fall and winter, moose consume large quantities of willow, birch, and aspen twigs. A moose is a giant twig-eater that produces moose nuggets (droppings). which are varnished and sold in our finer gift shops. During the summer moose feed on vegetation in shallow ponds, and the leaves of birch, willow, and aspen. Moose don't have any upper front teeth. Many sourdoughs don't either.

More people hunt moose than any other of Alaska's big game species. Alaskans and nonresidents annually harvest approximately 6,000-to-8,000 moose. An average bull provides about 500 pounds of meat. Moose meat is very low in fat and high in protein, making it much more nutritious than beef. Biologists estimate that there are roughly 155,000 moose in Alaska. Many more moose, cows, calves and bulls are killed by their predators, bears and wolves, than by hunters.

Bison –In 1928, 23 bison were shipped from the National Bison Range in Montana to Delta Junction and released. In 1996, there were roughly 1,000 bison in Alaska. The largest land animal in North America, bison can weigh more than a ton and stand six feet at the shoulder. Even though they may appear slow and clumsy, they have great endurance and can run as fast as 32 mph. Alaskan bison have been known to live up to 20 years. In the winter, bison require windblown areas that keep forage free of snow.

Bison cows usually give birth to a single calf in the spring. Bison calves are able to stand when only 30 minutes old. Within three hours of birth, they can run and kick their hind legs in the air. After about six days, calves start grazing.

Dall sheep are white mammals with amber horns, yellow eyes, and black noses and feet. Males weigh about 200 pounds and both sexes stand between three and three-and-a-half feet high at the shoulders. The horn clashing for which rams are so well known does not result from fights over ewes, but rather is a means of establishing a social hierarchy. Biologists estimate there are about 40,000 to 50,000 Dall sheep in Alaska.

Lambs are born in late May or early June. As the time to give birth approaches, ewes seek solitude and protection from predators in the most rugged cliffs available. Ewes bear a single lamb, and the ewe-lamb pairs remain together in steep terrain until the lambs are strong enough to travel.

Wolves – About 7,500 wolves live in Alaska. They range in color from black to nearly white, with every shade of gray, tan and even "blue" between these extremes. Most adult male wolves weigh from 85 to 115 pounds, but occasionally reach 145 pounds.

Wolves usually live in packs of about six or seven animals; however, a pack may have 30 or more wolves. Wolves are predators and, in most of Alaska, moose, caribou, and Dall sheep are their primary food. A pack may kill a moose every few days during the winter. At other times, they may go for several days with almost no food. On the average, each wolf eats about 12 moose or 36 caribou a year.

Wolf litters average about five pups, which are usually born in dens dug deep into well-drained soil. Wolves reach adult size by about one year of age and generally live about six years.

Northern HUMOR

- ☛ Alaska does have the customary four seasons: June, July, August, and winter. However, some folks still insist we only have two, nine months of winter and three months of poor skiing and dog-sledding.
- ☛ When you hear someone talking about the "Big One," you don't know if they're talking about Mt. McKinley, the earthquake, or the fish that just got away.
- ☛ I walked over to visit my neighbor Sam one afternoon. Seeing him looking lifeless in his rocking chair, I asked him, "How you doing, Sam?" His slow drawl answer was "Well, I didn't plan on doing anything today, and so far I am right on track."
- ☛ A confused sourdough is one who is in the habit of eating in his cabin and going outside to the outhouse, then visits his friends in the Lower 48 and is invited outside on the patio to eat and told to go inside to use the toilet.
- ☛ There is a difference between when you are in a rut, and when a bull moose is in rut. Both are considered dangerous.

- ☛ Don't drink downstream from a caribou crossing.
- ☛ If you are out fishing and a bear wants the fish you just caught, GIVE THE BEAR THE FISH.
- ☛ No matter how long you have been alone in the bush or how lonely you get, DO NOT accept a bear hug from a grizzly bear–they are barely bearable.
- ☛ The number one summer exercise of Alaskans is swatting mosquitoes. But be careful, some Alaskans get slapped silly by missing the mosquito too often.
- ☛ Many sourdoughs have attempted to capture a world class trophy mosquito. Anything over a three-inch wing span will qualify for the record book.
- ☛ Don't forget that the state flower is the forget-me-not.
- ☛ There is a difference between gold nuggets and moose nuggets. Moose nuggets are bigger and easier to find, but gold nuggets are worth a lot more.
- ☛ Mid-life crisis is when you stop growing in the polar regions ... and begin expanding in the equator.
- ☛ Don't get hung up on dress code here in Alaska, you wear whatever it takes to keep you warm.
- ☛ Sometimes when you get chilled clear through to the bone, you have to go to the hot springs to thaw out.
- ☛ When your breath freezes in front of your face, you have to thaw out your words to hear what you said.
- ☛ Bunny boots are not boots made for bunnies.
- ☛ No matter how thirsty you get, don't eat the yellow snow.
- ☛ Everyone knows that it doesn't cost a lot to live in Alaska-just to enjoy it.

Humorous Questions asked at the Visitors Bureau, in Fairbanks:

- ☛ "What time do they turn on the Northern Lights?"
- ☛ "Is this where I get the bus to the top of Mt. McKinley?"
- ☛ "Can you see all of Alaska in three days?"
- ☛ Lady: "How much does Mt. McKinley weigh?" Clerk: "Is that with or without snow and trees?" Lady: "Gee, … I never thought about that!"
- ☛ Over the phone: "We plan on coming to Fairbanks in July, how much snow is on the ground?"
- ☛ "If they know there's going to be a sunny day at Denali, do they issue a statewide alert or something?"
- ☛ "Isn't it noisy for people who live near the pipeline, with all of those barrels of oil rolling down the pipeline every day?"
- ☛ "Can we drive to Nome and Barrow?"
- ☛ "Where can we go to see fish jumping into bears' mouths?"
- ☛ "When do they let the animals out in Denali?"
- ☛ "Is it safe to camp out during my menstrual period?"
- ☛ "What is the total mileage of all the rivers and streams in Alaska?"
- ☛ "Where can we see polar bears in the area?"
- ☛ "How many bears are on the Chilkoot Trail?"
- ☛ Lady: "What advice would you give a person who wants to move to Alaska?" Clerk: "Well… where are you going to move to?" Lady: "I want to live in the brush!"
- ☛ "What kind of currency do you use, and what's the exchange rate?"
- ☛ "Where can we see Eskimos dancing?"
- ☛ "Can we take a train from Fairbanks to Seattle?"

- ☛ "Do you have Mounties that patrol the highway?"
- ☛ "When the sun shines all night, how do you know when to go to sleep?"

Questions From Valdez Visitors Bureau:

- ☛ "How fast was Bligh Reef going when it hit the Exxon Valdez?"
- ☛ "How much is postage to the States?"
- ☛ "When do caribou turn into moose?"
- ☛ "Where do you store all those barrels after the oil reaches Valdez?"
- ☛ "What kind of currency do you take?"
- ☛ "Do your hotels have running water?"
- ☛ "How do you get around in the winter in Valdez, dog sled?"
- ☛ "What year was the 1964 earthquake?"
- ☛ "I know all the snow melts, but where does all that white stuff go?"

Alaskan Tall Tales

The Old Native Trapper

By Bill Hamilton

I bumped into an old Native trapper along the upper Kobuk River one morning. He was the happiest looking specimen I had seen for a month of Sundays. The very essence of optimism radiated from his unshaven face, a smile like the wave on a rain barrel. It was a clear, crisp October morning and the bewhiskered old gentleman was walking down the mountainside with no shirt on.

"Seems sorta cool to be out here without a shirt," I said, shivering at the sight of him.

"Yuh," he grinned, "take off shirt to tie up hand."

"How'd you hurt your hand?" I noticed blood oozing through the big awkward bandage.

"Picking splinter out of hand when rock I stand on turn over-I fall, and cut a few fingers."

"Well, how did you get the splinter in your hand?"

"Shovel handle break-I keep on using."

"What were you shoveling for in the frozen ground?"

"Dig-grave, to bury family cat."

"What caused the cat to die?"

"He eat-too much charred dog meat."

"How did the dog meat get charred?"

"Dog team burn up, when cabin burn down."

"What caused your home to burn?"

"Still, he explode–turn stove over."

"Well, why were you making moonshine up here in the hills anyway?"

"Need fire water to keep up spirits, since wife leave."

"Where did your wife go?"

"She run off with fighter pilot, who up here on sheep hunt."

"Well, Mister," I asked in amazement, "How on earth can you look so pleasant and seem so optimistic after all these misfortunes?"

"Stranger," he said, still smiling, "I am all time much happy to know that long as we have one man in US Air Force with guts enough to live with that woman, any enemy ain't got a chance."

Bigger and Better

A few years ago a sourdough was in the club car of a train heading for Florida. A long, bow-legged fellow came in and sat down next to a youngster across from the sourdough.

"Pardner," said the bow-legged fellow, "where you from?"

"Kentucky," the youngster replied.

"Well, I'm from Texas," he retorted, "Greatest state in the union. You can put Kentucky and all of New England in just a little old corner of Texas…land area of 263,644 square miles, greatest state in the union."

Then the sourdough piped up. "Pardon me, pardner," he said to the Texan. "I'm from little old Alaska. Youngest state in the union, 588,400 square miles. One-fifth the size of the whole United States, twice the size of Texas. Greatest state in the union."

The Texan blinked at him, then turned back to the youngster. "As I was saying," he said, "you can't mention a thing that Texas ain't got. We got 400 miles of sea coast, you know, and..."

"Pardon me, pardner," the Alaskan said, "we got 4,750 miles of coast line, our shores are washed by two oceans, one sea, straits, gulfs, and God knows how many bays. We got..."

"Now take our mountains," Tex said. "There's Capitan in the Guadelunes, 9,020 feet high. That makes her about 5,000 feet higher than anything you got in Kentucky and..."

"Why, son," said the Alaskan, "that's just a little old hill. If you want a he-mountain, why don't you take old McKinley, 20,300 feet high. That makes her about 11,280 feet higher than anything you've got in…what's the name of that state again?..."

"And," Texas went on, "There's the old Rio Grande. What a river!"

"And," the Sourdough piped in, "there's the old Yukon, 2,000 miles long, and you'll never see the day that you can jump across."

By this time the Texan was foaming at the mouth, and then he turned toward the Alaskan stating, "We got oil, and gas, and gold, and silver, and mercury and lead and…"

"And," the Alaskan said, "we got oil, gold, silver, copper, tin, lead, platinum, pellacium, antimony, tungsten, coal, marble, glosum, sulphur, pitchblende, and fish and…"

"And," said Tex, "there ain't anything we can't grow. You ever see a Texas watermelon? Biggest thing you ever saw."

"Yeah," the sourdough responded, "bout half the size of a Matanuska Valley cabbage. Richest land in the world that Matanuska Valley land. It's..."

"But what we're really noted for," Tex piped back, "is our men. Takes real men to live in Texas. You ever heard of them 'blue northers' that whip through the Panhandle?"

"Yeah," the Alaskan replied, "They're just baby williwaws we send down for seasoning. When they get where they can break 100 miles an hour, they come back to Alaska to work out with some real men."

After that, the old Alaskan grinned at the youngster and got up to leave. Just as he disappeared from sight, the Texan again turned toward the youngster and whispered, "Them Alaskans! If they ain't the biggest-mouthed, loudest bunch of braggarts I ever heard. Why we ever let 'em in the union, I don't know!"

– "From the Louisville Courier"

Sam & his Fuzzy Little Critter

I think too much pot has affected his brain.

My neighbor Sam is different, he considers himself to be smarter than the average bear, but you judge for yourself. Sam is a budding entrepreneur. He swore me to secrecy the other day before telling me about his present brainstorm: creating the ultimate in home security systems. But, I now feel is my duty to my fellow Americans to warn the world before these cross breed devils become a reality in every home.

Here is what Sam confided to me. "I am attempting to breed wolverines with Tasmanian devils. The wolverine is noted for its killer instinct, strength, and ferocity. The Tasmanian devil is nocturnal, and widely known for its savageness, and viciousness, as well as being one of the smelliest, worst-tempered animals on earth. The cub, the offspring of that union, is what I want to sell to the homeowners, worldwide, for a modest sum."

Sam related his sales pitch: "No crook or unwanted guest would survive an encounter with one of these fierce fighting critters guarding your home."

To the Customers a WARNING tag on it's collar will read: "This fuzzy little critter may take a little getting used to. Feed it well, and DO NOT make it angry! You should not expect your new pet to be overly cuddly and friendly. That's not its job. This critter exists for the sole purpose of keeping intruders out. If you want cuddly and friendly, get a cat."

Sam did confess to minor delays, although it will give the world time to prepare for the arrival of these devils. His first challenge is to determine when the wolverine and the Tasmanian devil are in simultaneous amorous moods. The next problem is getting them to mate without killing each other.

I had to shake my head, I walked back to my cabin and locked the door.

Jake, my Other Neighbor

I thought he had frozen into an icicle.

One frosty midwinter evening, I was returning from a hurried trip to the outhouse when I spotted Jake out in front of his log cabin. Dressed in nothing but his long johns and mukluks, he stood like a statue, staring up at the sky and the Northern Lights as they performed overhead. So I walked over to see if he had gone bonkers, or what could possess him to stand out in the cold, dressed in long johns.

His greeting words to me were: "Neighbor, I've traveled

this state over-been to the Eskimo Olympics and three State Fairs–I ran in the Iditarod and made two trips to Alaskaland–I've been on the Riverboat Discovery, and I've seen Mt. McKinley from three sides–I've been on seven moose hunts and on two whale sightings–I've been to a caribou barbecue and a duck-plucking contest–I've fished in the Salmon Derby, and I've picked up gold nuggets the size of blueberries–but I ain't never in all my travels, ever seen anything as pretty as Miss Aurora dancing."

Herman the Hermit
Spends an Exotic Evening
By Don Elbert

Midway into one of Alaska's bitter cold, dark, winters Herman, a lone and lonesome sourdough, who lives 75 dogsled miles from the closest village, gets pretty bored. When it's so cold that it takes raw courage to leave the cabin, Sam eats only one small meal a day to cut his trips to the outhouse down to a bare minimum. In an effort to keep his sanity and not fall off the deep end, Sam has devised a way to break the monotony and boredom.

An exotic evening of bubble bathing is what he has dreamed up, something a little more exciting than just watching the frost creep up the inside walls of his 12X16 foot log cabin, or watching his toe nails grow. He'll start by preparing for his only meal, lunch, a steaming bowl of one of the north's staples, beans and a slice of sourdough bread. Following lunch, he'll take a nap. Upon awakening, he'll bundle up in his parka and venture out to get the big old laundry tub from under the front steps, and place it on the Yukon stove. He'll walk out a ways, and commence hauling in clean, white snow, not the yellow-tinted snow by the doghouse.

Once the tub is full of snow, he'll haul in more wood and stoke the stove until it turns a cherry red, and the snow starts to melt. Now he can relax, letting his lunch settle, and nature take its course. By evening time the snow, now nice hot water, will be ready for his tired body (he got tired out hauling in firewood and carrying in all that snow).

Now he's ready for the all-day-long-anticipated bubble bath, the ultimate in remote cabin bathing. But before entering the tub to relax for the evening, he'll strip, even removing his crusty long johns, and that is something he usually does not do until spring. He climbs in the tub and lathers all up, lies back and relaxes, enjoying the soothing, calming, therapeutic feeling of the warm bath water. If he times everything just right (starting from lunch), the bubbles ought to start appearing about now. Sam counts the bubbles for a while, he spears some and squashes others, all the while attempting to get one to fly like a balloon. Out in the bush, on a cold night, this is as entertaining as life can get. Sam's face glows, showing his enjoyment of the finer things in life. It is entirely possible for Sam to spend hours of enchantment in the tub, relaxing, thawing, meditating, and watching the bubbles pop, at least till the water turns cold and the bubbles stop.

The Day Fred Exploded

By Don Elbert

The thermometer froze on 53 degrees below zero that Monday morning in Fairbanks, and I was late for work. I had spent the best part of an hour cuddled up inside my parka, trying without success to breathe life into my frozen car. The cold had crept in under my wooly long johns, causing my body to stiffen near straight as a willow tree. Then, like a hand grenade going off, the morning silence was shattered. Peering through the dense fog, I made out the cause of the ruckus, my irritable neighbor. Now, right up front, I want you to know that Fred's temper is attached by a short fuse, and he had exploded! He was out in his fire engine red stocking cap, and white bunny boots, kicking rock-size dents in the front fender of his vintage pickup truck and screaming in a voice that could be heard in Seattle. Just the heat alone, radiating from his sizzling words, melted a hole right through the center of that ice fog.

Quote: "You dad-burned no-account, decrepit pile of dented scrap metal trash, good for nothing bucket of twisted, cross-threaded bolts. You big pile of faded blue metallic poop, froze-up ice cube hunk of dilapidated, rusted, cantankerous, junk iron. I'm going to poke my double barreled, 12-gauge shotgun down the rusty throat of your leaking radiator and blow your non-cranking rod-bearing plum out the back of your Swiss-cheese looking tail pipe. Then I gonna drag your worthless, bent frame to the bone yard."

I listened with compassion – and understood – then I replied,

"Yo, Fred, my car won't start either."

The Wisdom of a Survivor

- ☛ Listen to advice from older sourdoughs: there is no advantage to making the same mistakes that gave them their premature gray hairs.
- ☛ The best preparation against sub-zero weather is long-handled underwear, which features a trap door.
- ☛ Know when to shovel the snow off your roof, before the roof caves in.
- ☛ Stoke your wood-burning Yukon stove so it will last all night.
- ☛ Everybody falls down in the snow occasionally…the difference between living or freezing is how long it takes you to get up.
- ☛ The weather is always fine for the fellow who is appropriately dressed.
- ☛ Persistence usually pays off…enough little strokes will chop down the largest tree.
- ☛ Don't wait until your ears are frostbitten before raising the hood of your parka.
- ☛ No mattress makes one sleep so soundly as fatigue from a hard day's work.
- ☛ Boys and girls, think about what you're going to look like when you grow up. If you want lusterless eyes that look like burned holes in a rug…cheeks with the crimson hue of an Alaska sunset…and a nose resembling a frozen sweet potato–drink whiskey.
- ☛ It's summertime and you learn never to tell your kids, "Be home by dark!"
- ☛ Don't argue: Always give up your blueberry patch to visiting bears.

The Gospel According to A Sourdough

1. Thou shalt not wander through bear country with bacon breath, or with anyone who can run faster than you.
2. Thou shalt not practice deep breathing while in the outhouse.
3. Thou shalt not linger outside, half-naked, during mosquito season.
4. Thou shalt not pan for gold in another man's sluice box.
5. Thou shalt not try to take the antlers off a moose without his permission.
6. Thou shalt not build a roaring fire inside your igloo.
7. Thou shalt not swipe your neighbor’s smoked salmon.
8. Thou shalt not bite off more whale blubber than you can chew.
9. Thou shalt not delay cutting firewood till you are shivering, and if you do, don't covet your neighbor's woodpile.
10. Thou shalt not neglect warm clothing to ward off frost-bite.
11. Thou shalt not seek a bear hug from a grizzly bear.
12. Thou shalt not attempt to walk on water, unless it's frozen.

The Alaska Quiz:

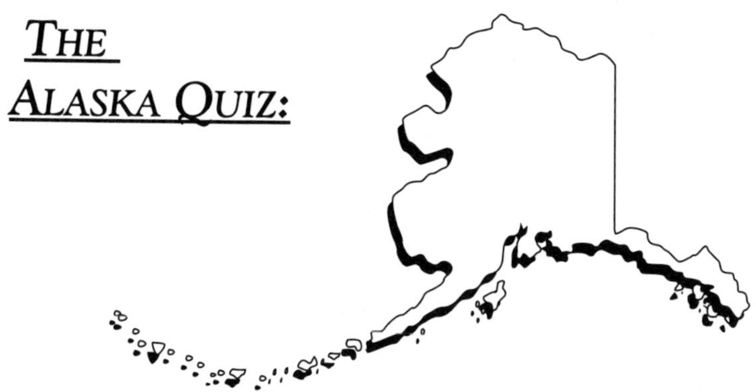

1. What is the largest (by weight) land mammal in the state of Alaska? Be careful, most people guess wrong.
2. What are the four basic colors seen in the Aurora Borealis?
3. What is Alaska's most popular guessing game?
4. How can anything as big and majestic as Mt. McKinley be hidden from view for three-fourths of the summer?
5. Which one of these three are not found in alaska, ice worms, Penguins, polar bears?
6. How many stars are on the Alaska flag?
7. How can it be Saturday on Alaska's Little Diomede Island and Sunday on the Big Diomede Island just two and one half miles away?
8. What are the two states that have less population than Alaska?
9. How many ounces are in a pound of gold?
10. How many gallons constitute a barrel of oil flowing through the pipeline?
11. Do more earthquakes occur in Alaska or California?
12. Who can run faster, a brown bear or a horse?

Answers on next page.

Answers To The Quiz:

1 Bison (2000 lbs.) — Moose (1500 lbs.)
Brown bear (1400 lbs.) – Polar bear (1400 lbs.)
2. Green is the common color, with various shades of white, red, and blue mixed in to make the different hues of flickering streamers that are the Northern Lights.
3. The Nenana Ice Classic. You guess and bet on the day, hour and minute the Tanana River Ice goes out.
4. Clouds.
5. Penguins live in Antarctic. If you see one in Alaska, it's a tourist just visiting.
6. Eight gold stars on a field of blue.
7. The International Date Line separates the two islands.
8. Wyoming and Vermont.
9. Twelve Troy ounces.
10. Forty-two gallons is the standard for a barrel of oil.
11. Alaska.
12. A brown bear can outrun a horse. A charging brown bear can sprint up to 40 miles an hour for a short distance.

The Alaska Blessing

May your woodpile last all winter,
May your hands and toes stay warm,
May your mukluks walk in safety,
May God bless and keep you from harm.

May your cabin be warm and cozy,
May your dog team never fail,
May the good Lord keep your pantry full,
Good health and blessings on the trail.

May the winter winds be at your back,
May the summer sun warm your face,
May your needs be few, your blessings many,
May God enrich your life with grace.

The Author

Don Elbert moved from Seattle to Alaska in 1947 when he was 13 years old to help his dad farm a 100-acre homestead. He learned how to clear land, grow potatoes, cut firewood, melt snow for water, and survive in a cold climate.

For the past 52 years, Don has experienced the essence of Alaska by climbing its mountains and walking through its valleys. Don retired after 31 years as a heavy equipment mechanic, and still lives on one acre of the original homestead near Fairbanks with his wife Elaine. They raised five children and now have 15 grandchildren. Over the years Don has panned for gold, boated and fished it's rivers, hunted and trapped it's game, and repaired a lot of equipment here in Alaska.

Don learned to love this land, like his father did before him. This book is his way to share with you some of the best of the thrills and chills that, for him, made life worth living in the far north.

Other books by Don Elbert
Fascinating History, Facts & Fun about Alaska
First edition published in 1995.

Alaska the Cold Truth-published in 1996.

And next to be published-***Alaska Exposed***